BREAD OR BLOOD

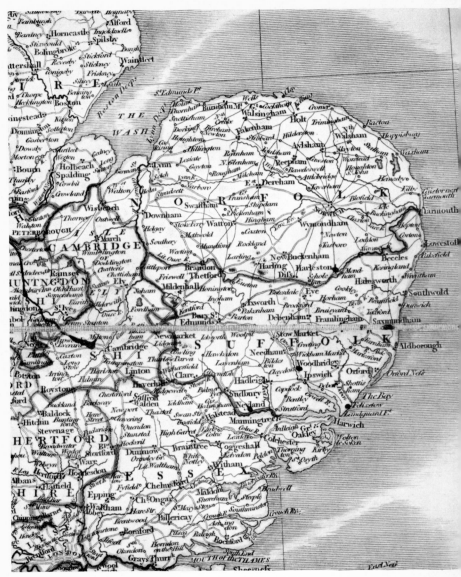

East Anglia from *A New and Accurate Description of all the direct and principle Cross Roads in Great Britain* by Daniel Paterson, 15th edition, London, 1811.

BREAD OR BLOOD

A STUDY OF THE AGRARIAN RIOTS
IN EAST ANGLIA IN 1816

by

A. J. PEACOCK

with a foreword by

E. P. THOMPSON

LONDON
VICTOR GOLLANCZ LTD
1965

MADE AND PRINTED IN GREAT BRITAIN BY
THE GARDEN CITY PRESS LIMITED
LETCHWORTH, HERTFORDSHIRE

"The surest way to prevent seditions, if the times do bear it, is to take away the matter of them . . . the rebellions of the belly are worst."

—Lord Bacon

"They are people in *want*. They are people who have *nothing to lose*, except their lives; and of these they think little, seeing that they have so little enjoyment of them. . . . 'Tis *food* they want; and I know from my own observation, and I have a hundred times stated the fact, that, even before this terrible distress came upon us, the labouring people had not *half a sufficiency* of food."

—William Cobbett

"The process of obtaining relief or redress by application first to a parish officer, and afterwards to a magistrate is so plain, so easy and so generally understood, that there can be no plea for resorting to any other means."

—The Rev. George Stone
at the Bury Quarter Sessions, July 1816

"Here I am, between Earth and Sky—so help me God. I would sooner loose my life than go home as I am. Bread I want and Bread I will have."

—William Dawson,
one of the rioters at Upwell

"I might as well be hanged as starved."

—Richard Rutter,
a rioter at Ely

To my parents
whose predecessors, I strongly
suspect, were among
the rioters.

INTRODUCTION

THIS LITTLE BOOK is the result of a chance discovery of documents relating to the Ely and Littleport riots that had only just been deposited in the Cambridgeshire Record Office. These led me to hitherto unused material in the Treasury Solicitor's Papers at the Public Record Office. The latter contained a great amount of detail about the actual course of the rebellion and the subsequent trials and enabled me to build up what I think is a comprehensive account of what happened in East Anglia during the first half of 1816. I have given this story in detail, perhaps too much detail, in the second part of the book. Whatever is known about the *dramatis personae* I have also included either in the text or appendices. One of the reasons for doing this is the assumption that there may be other documents in parish records and so on that could be used to throw more light on some of the more obscure and bizarre incidents, in which case the minutiae of the story will be useful to students.

With one exception the documents above told little about the actual conditions of the labourers in 1816. The first part of the book therefore deals with the background to the events of that year. Parts of the story are already well known, as are many of the quotations used. They have been chosen because their familiarity is the result of their being so pertinent. Young on enclosure and Crabbe on the workhouse, for instance, can hardly be bettered.

All the shortcomings in the book and any errors of interpretation or fact are entirely my responsibility, but I must acknowledge the special debt I owe to Mr. E. P. Thompson whose great book appeared while I was preparing my material. Mr. Thompson read the MS. and went to great lengths to help me. I should also like to thank Mr. Rex Russell, of the University of Hull, for his help and interest; Mr. W. E. Tate, of the University of Leeds; Mr. Thurley and Mr. Willis, of the Cambridge

Reference Library, who were always incredibly helpful; Mrs.
Nancy Catchpole; Mr. Tim Evens; Miss Maureen Robson; Mr.
Farrer, the Cambridge County Archivist; and Miss Margaret
Atkinson, who typed the script.

A. J. PEACOCK

York Educational Settlement
July 1964

FOREWORD

ENGLAND HAS GENERALLY succeeded in exporting her agrarian wars. Through much of the eighteenth and nineteenth centuries Ireland was the great market. Meanwhile, at home, the gentry rode imperturbably to church or to hounds, and the ladies drove on their social calls. English *chateaux* did not go up in flames; English bailiffs (in England at least) did not spur home before dusk for fear of the sniper in the hedgerow.

By the end of the eighteenth century English agriculture was a most profitable capitalist industry—aggressive, expansionist, receptive to technological innovations. The expansion was bought at a heavy social cost: against the increased yield of the enclosed acres we must set the break-up of the traditional village community. During the French wars the landowners and farming tenants gained inflated profits, and most of all in years of mediocre harvest when they were doubly compensated in rising prices for the falling-away in yield. In these profits the rural labourers had no share.

Why did they submit? How did the gentry succeed in extorting from them not only their labour but also a sullen deference? Were they weakened by a continual haemorrhage from the countryside of the young and the rebellious, into the manufacturing districts or to London or the Army? Were they betrayed from within by fatalism? Was the rule of law in the village too proximate and too powerful, with its comprehensive control over economic, spiritual, and moral life—over employment, over poor relief and settlement, over their cottages, over the pulpit, the bridewell and the gallows?

They did not always submit, of course. The eighteenth century saw many food "riots"—direct actions to reduce prices and to levy money from the wealthy. In this place and in that, enclosure was resisted. The last years of the century saw attempts to raise wages by rural trade unions—attempts which have rarely left more record than an entry in the indictments at Quarter Sessions, or the laconic reports in the Press as to their outcome:

At Norfolk assizes, several labourers in agriculture were tried for having assembled and conspired to compel their masters to raise their wages. The prisoners were all found guilty, and sentenced to a year's imprisonment . . . (September, 1800).

It was only after the French wars, when the enclosers and their lawyers were surfeited, when prices fell from their artificial heaven, and when some demobilised labourers walked or hitched on carts back to their home villages, that anything approaching a general agrarian disturbance took place. The "Ely Riots", which Mr. Peacock describes (and it is one of the many merits of his book that we must refer to them henceforward as the "East Anglian Riots", since he shows them to have been much more extensive than historians had supposed), partake in many features of the food riots and forced levies of the previous century. In other features—the demand for a minimum wage, the sporadic expression of social and political demands, the inchoate reaching out towards organisation—they anticipate the "last labourers' revolt" of 1830, and even the trade unionism and radicalism of later years, in which East Anglia has always played so prominent a part.

This is an important episode in East Anglian history, of course. But it is an important episode in English history more generally. The sources which Mr. Peacock has uncovered throw light upon the life of the rural labourer in a period which has hitherto been obscure. The riots give us a section of rural history, enabling us to understand better, not only the springs of revolt, but also the resources of Law and Order, as Mr. Peacock moves us forward to his final chapter where, at the Ely Special Assizes, judges, clergy and gentry, as in some savage Brechtian climax, reduce the countryside to deference once more. Those who are interested in the history of the common people will read this book anyway. Those who sentimentalise Regency England need to read it most of all.

E.P.T.

CHAPTER ONE

IN THE EARLY summer of 1816 England was surprised and alarmed by the news that the agricultural labourers of East Anglia had come out in revolt. Conditions had worsened since the ending of the Napoleonic wars, and riots and disturbances were everyday occurrences in the towns. The rural population, however, had been regarded as supine, lethargic and, although prone to riot on a small scale, never likely or capable of taking part in a movement serious enough to cause a real threat to society.

The train of events that ended in a specially staged trial of the rioters at Ely and Littleport began in 1815. As conditions worsened, the incidents increased in number. They also altered in character. At first there were attacks on property (usually farm implements) in remote villages. Later, when a really serious rise in the price of bread started, there were attacks on both property and persons in the few large towns in the area—Bury St. Edmunds first, then Brandon, Norwich and Downham Market. Last of all the labourers of Littleport broke out in rebellion on 21st May. The following day they marched to Ely, where they enlisted the aid of the locals and terrorised the millers and magistrates, forcing the latter to capitulate and agree to their demands. Later they took part in an unequal pitched battle with the military in which a life was lost. Five more of their number were eventually executed, dozens of them were transported, and the area was pacified for the next twenty or thirty years.

The rising of the East Anglian labourers was only one, although in many ways the most significant, of the troubles of 1816. The agricultural labourer was always the last to bestir himself—this is also true of 1830 and the early 'seventies when the next real movements took place—and when he did so it was a real indication of the deplorable conditions prevailing at the time, whether they were political, social or economic. Samuel Bamford began a chapter of his *Passages in the Life of a Radical* by simply listing the stormy events of the early part of 1816.

It is a matter of history, that whilst the laurels were yet cool on the brows of our victorious soldiers on their second occupation of Paris, the elements of convulsion were at work amongst the masses of our labouring population; and that a series of disturbances commenced with the introduction of the Corn Bill in 1815, and continued with short intervals, until the close of the year 1816. In London and Westminster riots ensued, and were continued for several days, whilst the bill was discussed; at Bridport, there were riots on account of the high price of bread; at Biddeford there were similar disturbances to prevent the exportation of grain; at Bury, by the unemployed, to destroy machinery; at Ely, not suppressed without bloodshed; at Newcastle-on-Tyne, by colliers and others; at Glasgow, where blood was shed, on account of soup kitchens; at Preston, by unemployed weavers; at Nottingham, by Luddites, who destroyed thirty frames; at Methyr-Tydville, on a reduction of wages; at Birmingham, by the unemployed; at Walsall, by the distressed; and December 7th, 1816, at Dundee, where, owing to the high price of meal, upwards of one hundred shops were plundered.[1]

Whereas considerable attention has been paid to many of the incidents mentioned by Bamford, the events in East Anglia have by and large been ignored by historians. A few brief, contemporary accounts were published,[2] and on these almost every subsequent account has been based,[3] but they are misleading in the extreme. Without exception they were wrong in detail, give the impression that the troubles were of short duration and, moreover, were written as warnings to other would-be rioters. None of them had any more sympathy for the labourers than did the Press of the time. They were represented simply as "banditti" and "pot valiant fenmen" who were receiving "great wages" and who rioted for rioting's sake. None of this was true. The revolt was a revolt of desperate men; the criticisms were those of a class which had divested itself of the responsibilities it once had to the poor and oppressed.

The events and the attitudes of 1816 must be seen against the background of a society in transition. The years in which the labourers who rebelled grew up were years in which Britain completed the change-over from "the old moral economy" to the "economy of the free market",[4] and years in which the rich got ostentatiously richer, but the poor became poorer. In the towns this resulted in the creation of an industrial proletariat and a hardening of class attitudes, and was achieved largely by "the abrogation or repeal of 'paternalist' legislation covering apprentice-

ship, wage-regulation, or conditions in industry".[5] The leaders
of the community shed the last of their age-old obligations towards the poorer sections of society, who became mere wage
labourers, dependent for employment and sustenance on the
whims of the manufacturers. The once "deserving" became the
"designing" poor, an essential, if regrettable, part of the body
politic.

In the countryside the change-over was no less drastic. The
labourer became a landless worker after enclosure, and farming
rapidly became capitalistic, with the relations between worker
and employer similar to that in the towns. Ideas of a "just wage"
fixed and enforced by the J.P.s were thrown over and the hind
was turned out of his master's house and left to fend for himself. The laws protecting property were made even more strin-
gent, and the Poor Laws harsher.

What Cobbett called "Scotch feelosofy" and the Hammonds the
"spirit of the age" was endorsed as heartily by landowners as by
manufacturers. But whereas it fitted the conditions of the Industrial
Revolution like a glove, in agriculture it contested (at best) with
older paternalist traditions (the squire's duty to his labourers) and
with the tradition of earnings based on need (the older customs of
differentials according to age, marital status, children, etc., which
were perpetuated under the Speenhamland system of poor relief);
while (at worst) it was reinforced by the feudal arrogance of the
aristocracy towards the inferior labouring race.[6]

One of the most significant departures from the practices of
paternalistic society can be seen in the repeal of the legislation
against forestalling and engrossing at the end of the eighteenth
century. Politicians (who were out of sympathy with "the spirit
of the age") and some J.P.s fought against the disappearance,
but to no avail. However, offences of this nature "endured with
undiminished vigour . . . in popular tradition",[7] and any sudden
rise in prices would be put down to sharp practice and spark off
a riot against the millers, the shopkeepers, and the butchers.

Rioting was commonplace in the eighteenth and early nineteenth centuries and many more examples than those cited in
this book could be produced of the labourers violently campaign-
ing (for instance) for a reduction in prices. They were denied
political or legal redress and machine-breaking and rick-burning
was their only resort. In fact, it was an essential part "of the
methods of struggle" of the early working class, an acknowledged

form of "political" behaviour that Dr. Hobsbawm has referred
to as "collective bargaining by riot".[8] The bread-rioter was
popularly regarded on a par with the poacher. His actions were
not immoral; they corresponded to "an extraordinarily deep-
rooted pattern of behaviour and belief" and were legitimised by
"the assumptions of an older moral economy which taught the
immorality of any unfair method of forcing up the price of
provisions by profiteering upon the necessities of the people".[9]
Moreover "political" rioting was often effective, particularly in
places like Norwich.[10]

The poverty of the mass of labourers, artisans, and petty traders
of course disqualified them from participation in politics, and prevented effective access to the courts. The remedy of the property-
less and unenfranchised was to riot. Common grievance such as the
price of corn and the supposed malpractices of middlemen and
retailers were a perennial source of disturbances. The inadequacy
of the forces of law and order made the mob something to be feared
by the mightiest, and even formed a fairly effective check on petty
abuses. In London a duke dare not walk alone through the streets
in his usual dress; and in the countryside proprietors like Sir John
Heathcote, whose attempt to enclose a common pasture was
frustrated by a mob who peremptorily threw down his fences, and
Lord Gage, who was hard put to it to restrain the colliers of the
Forest of Dean from exercising their supposed right to dig coal on
his land, knew from experience the limitations of their authority.[11]

The East Anglian riots of 1816 corresponded exactly to this
"pattern of behaviour and belief". There *was* a sudden rise in
prices prior to the outbreak, and millers and shopkeepers were
among the chief objects of the rioters. The crowd at Brandon, for
instance, said "they wanted their rights . . . *Cheap Bread, a
Cheap Loaf and Provisions cheaper*",[12] and a Mr. Norman, a
miller, was accused of forcing up the price of flour. At Ely,
Norwich and Downham Market mills were broken into, millers
and butchers attacked and food distributed among the crowd.
"We deem the miller as big a rogue as you farmers," the
labourers of Ashill announced, "for [as you] raise [wheat] 1s. per
Comb. He will . . . raise [it] 2d. per stone."[13]

The transition described above, necessary to an evolving industrial society, had an alleged political as well as an economic
justification. The prevailing "slave complex" that Mr. Whiteley
has written about[14] made it certain that the superior orders

would not be unduly alarmed at the sufferings of the poor, but they sanctioned oppression by affecting to see in them a potential revolutionary mass liable to emulate the continentals and take up arms against the established order.

In the early days of the French Revolution there had existed an obvious antagonism between the old established society and the representatives of the new, between the "oligarchy of land and commerce and the manufacturers and petty gentry".[15] From this the labourers might conceivably have benefited, as they did when Shaftesbury championed the town labourers and the manufacturers took up the cause of the rural workers later on, if developments had continued on their "natural course". "The 'natural' alliance between an impatient radically-minded industrial bourgeoisie and a formative proletariat was broken [however] as soon as it was formed."[16] Manufacturers had once been prominent in reform movements, but the threat of Jacobinism and the egalitarian doctrines of *The Rights of Man* "*consolidated* Old Corruption by uniting landowners and manufacturers in a common panic".

Alarmed at the French example, and in the patriotic fervour of war, the aristocracy and the manufacturers made common cause. The English *ancien régime* received a new lease of life, not only in national affairs, but also in the perpetuation of the antique corporations which misgoverned the swelling industrial towns.[17]

The threat of revolution was reckoned to come mainly from the growing mass of industrial workers in the towns, but the rural labourers were nevertheless regarded with suspicion, if not the same fear, and they suffered in the same way as did the townspeople. The "threat" to the sanctity of private property, and the need for its protection at all costs, justified the harsh laws and spring guns used against the poachers. Ideology was added to self interest, and turning the hind into a mere wage labourer came to be "public spirited policy". Poets like Oliver Goldsmith, and writers like the Reverend David Davies, and even Arthur Young, may have pointed out the evil effects of enclosure, but they went unheeded. The commons once "the poor man's heritage for ages past" became "centres of indiscipline" to be taken over in the interests of society. The tyranny of the countryside became a sensible bulwark against a revolutionary peasantry who had somehow overcome their illiteracy

and had absorbed Paine's teachings in their entirety.[18] (Had they
managed to do so, they would have found ample justification for
much of their behaviour. "When the rich plunder the poor of
his rights," Paine said, "it becomes an example to the poor to
plunder the rich of his property.")[19]

There have been a number of very valuable studies of the
agricultural labourer during the eighteenth and nineteenth centuries, notably those by Hasbach,[20] and the Hammonds in *The
Village Labourer*. However, all of these have been studies
painted on a wide canvas, and much still remains to be told
about the conditions and attitudes of the rural workers at the
end of the Napoleonic wars. For that reason it would be as well,
before describing the actual course of the events of 1816, to look
again at the steps by which the labourers were reduced to the
level they were at on the eve of revolt. Most of those involved
were in their early thirties or late twenties and had grown up
during one of the blackest periods in the history of their class.

During the thirty or so years before 1816 the enclosing of open
fields and commons went ahead rapidly in almost every part of
East Anglia. Dr. Hasbach referred to the movement as "the last
act in the drama of proletarianisation".[21] Certainly it was the
most significant of the changes taking place : an overwhelming
demonstration to the labourer of his future rôle in society and
the way his "rights" could be ignored and taken away almost
at will. There are disputes about the extent to which he was
harmed through enclosure, and in some places his lot probably
improved, at least for a time, through increased work opportunities. That many *were* hurt in the way the Hammonds describe,
however, is certain; that the majority *considered* they were
wronged is beyond doubt. "You do as you like," wrote the
labourers of Ashill in the letter already quoted. "You rob the
poor of their common rights, plough the grass up that God send
to grow, that a poor man may feed a cow, Pig, Horse, nor Ass.
There is 5 or 6 of you have gotten all the whole of the land
in this parish in your own hands and you would wish to be rich
and starve all the other part of the poor of the parish."

The Board of Agriculture surveyed most of the counties of
England twice during the period 1790 to 1816, and a comparison of the earlier and later surveys gives a clear picture of the
magnitude of the enclosure movement in East Anglia. Thomas

Stone, for instance, reported in 1793 that there were "130,000 acres of commonable meadows, commons and common fields" in Huntingdon,[22] while his successor stated that "most of the best commons in the county are now enclosed . . ."[23] Essex had long been enclosed, but the two reports for Cambridgeshire show a similar picture to that in Huntingdon. Charles Vancouver said that in 1794 there were still 132,000 acres of open field arable land compared with only 15,000 enclosed arable,[24] while William Gooch showed that the areas under open field and common had been greatly lessened by 1807.[25] Nathaniel Kent, writing of Norfolk in 1796, said that about a quarter of the arable area of the county was tilled on the common or open-field system,[26] while Arthur Young, a few years later, indicated that although quite a lot still remained, considerable inroads had been made by enclosure.[27]

Enclosures were not done swiftly and at one time. In many cases the time that elapsed between an Act and the actual award covered many years, during which the owners could have been kept waiting to see the outcome of their claims, although, perhaps, most were told unofficially what would happen very soon after they appeared before the Commissioners. This must have been an agonising experience for those whose future was in doubt. Any number of examples of East Anglian parishes in the position of uncertainty when the May riots of 1816 broke out can be found. At Woodstone (Hunts), for instance, the Act was passed in 1809 and the award not announced until 1821. Great Paxton and Toseland, in the same county, were the subject of an Act passed in 1811 but the inhabitants had to wait seven years for the award, while at Upton the process covered the five years between 1812 and '17. In Cambridgeshire an Enclosure Act including open field arable in Swaffham Prior was passed in 1805 and the award announced in 1814, while in the Norfolk parishes of Barford, Hedenham, Diss and Binham the awards were all published in the fateful year of 1816.[28] In Suffolk the story was the same. The people of Troston and Great Thurlow heard of Acts in 1806, but whereas in the former case the award was announced in the following year, the Great Thurlow award was delayed until 1825. At the trouble spot of Brandon the process was completed between 1807 and '10, and at Bury St. Edmunds between 1814 and '16. In West Suffolk as a whole the largest proportion of nineteenth-century enclosures took place between 1811 and 1818. At the beginning of 1816 no less than

twenty-five parishes for which Acts had been passed were awaiting the awards.[29] All this contributed to the fund of ill feeling
that erupted into violence in the summer.

In contrast to the casual way awards were often completed,
the speed with which the decision to enclose was made must
have impressed itself upon the populace. The process of enclosure
has often been described[30] and a decision to apply for an Act
could be sprung on the populace without any general discussion.
A Press announcement or a public notice on the church door
might be the first a cottager or small owner heard of an intended
enclosure, but once in Parliament the measures (except where
other large or powerful landowners objected) were rushed
through with almost indecent haste. The petition applying for
an Act for Bury St. Edmunds, for instance, was introduced and
referred to committee on the 18th November 1813. Leave to
bring in a Bill was given on 21st March 1814. It was read a
second time exactly a month later, reported on 16th May, agreed
to by the Lords on 16th June and given the Royal assent the
next day. The enclosure of Stoke Ferry, Wretton, Wereham and
Winnold (Norfolk), however, was a more complicated affair,
owing to the opposition of an interested party. The original petition was introduced in March 1815 but was thrown out because
it was wrongly drawn. It was reintroduced in April when a Mr.
Abraham Sewell petitioned against. It was read a third time on
5th May 1815 and passed the Lords with amendments favour-
ing Sewell a month later. The Commons agreed to the alterations
on the 12th June and the Royal assent was given two days later.
The Bill for enclosing Bradfield was introduced on 18th November 1813 and obtained the Royal assent on 17th June of the
next year.

In almost every enclosure the poorer sections of the community suffered either directly or indirectly. Small owners often
found the costs of fencing, hedging and ditching prohibitive and
had no alternative but to sell their land and become wage
labourers.[31] Arthur Young likened the process to stealing a man's
handkerchief and then employing him to embroider the new
owner's initials on it.

The classes below the small owners suffered most of all.
Tenants had no claim as such and were often deprived of their
land because of the landlord's desire for larger, more economic
holdings. "Cottagers, who occupied at a yearly rent the ancient
cottages to which common rights were attached, received no com-

pensation for the loss of rights which they only exercised as tenants. Squatters, who had encroached on the wastes and commons, and had not made good their titles by prescriptive occupation, were evicted."[32] It is true that there were many lenient Acts in which allotments and cottage gardens were set aside for the poor, but, according to Arthur Young, in what was certainly his most famous remark: "By nineteen Enclosure Acts out of twenty, the poor are injured, in some grossly injured . . . The poor in these parishes may say," he went on, *"Parliament may be tender of property; all I know is I had a cow, and an Act of Parliament has taken it from me."*[33] Gooch, writing of Abingdon Pigots (Cambs), had to submit "A very . . . melancholy account . . . formerly every poor man had a cow, some by right, others by permission"; now they had none. In Guilden Morden, he said, "there will be an end of cowkeeping amongst the poor, as in the neighbouring parish of Abington Pigots. The poor are therefore greatly alarmed and view the steps taken for enclosure with terror". Professor Chambers commented on the way these groups were ignored in practically every Act, and how difficult it would be to estimate the extent of their suffering.

Nothing however, is said of the lowest group of all, the cottage labourers with customary usage of the common; and nothing statistically can be said. Since they had no proprietary rights to defend they do not appear in the enclosure award . . . these landless or semi-landless workers, together with the small tenants who disappeared through consolidation, represent the real victims of enclosure . . .[34]

In Great Parndon (Essex) when 150 acres of common were enclosed in 1795, it was reckoned that as it "yielded no fuel of any kind . . . no allotment was made for it". Others were a little more fortunate. "Small allotments were made to the poor people who kept geese, &c., but they have been bought, except a single one, by the land proprietors."[35] In Harston (Cambs) enclosure deprived both tenants and owners of their land. "An acre . . . was allotted to each cottage, but as most of the cottages belonged to the owners of large estates, they laid the land to them instead of attaching it to the cottages; but where the cottages were the property of the occupiers of them, many have sold or let."[36] At Abington Pigots, after enclosure, "the whole parish belonged to one person, the rights had allotments assigned them, and were thrown to the farms".[37]

If the House of Commons Journals rarely mention opposition to enclosure, there is still evidence to be found of occasional resistance in the local Press of East Anglia. In the absence of an organised police force, numerous Associations for the Prosecution of Felons existed throughout the area. These offered to pay rewards to people informing on anyone found "guilty of crimes and misdemeanours . . . upon the properties of subscribers". A scale of rewards was drawn up and that of the Burnt Fen Association saying that, for information regarding the stealing of unthreshed corn or the "breaking down and stealing any Fences, or stealing any Turf, Wood, or other Firing or . . . any other offences not hereinfore enumerated", there would be "a reward of *One Guinea*",[38] suggests that opposition to enclosure was not unknown in that area.

There is little detailed information about the East Anglian labourer's resistance to enclosure to be found, nothing, for instance, to compare with the account of the Otmoor troubles in Oxfordshire. There is a report of a trial at the Norfolk Assizes in April 1815, however, in which William Mason, Edmund Chilley, Thomas Brock and Ann Rush were indicted for wilfully and maliciously damaging a fence erected after the awards made under the Lopham Enclosure Act were announced (an offence punishable by death).[39] The case is only briefly reported but is interesting because it produced a labourer courageous enough to put his people's views in court. "Mason addressed the court," it is said, "as champion of the rights of the poor, whose property he said the commons were. The Judge stated distinctly to the prisoners and to the Jury, however, that the poor had no such right as was asserted by the prisoner."[40] It is only fair to add that in this enclosure some 200 acres had been allotted either to or for the poor. Mason "his case being more aggravated from the part he took in the transaction was sentenced to *twelve months imprisonment*, and the three other prisoners were sentenced to *three months imprisonment each*".[41] At Feltwell during the riots of 1816 a crowd made a great show of first breaking a dam across a drain, after which they went "to Mr. Denton's land and there threw down part of a fence".[42]

The great loss of a cow to people like Mason is obvious; hardly less so was the right to take fuel from the commons. After having the right to gather enough for their domestic needs, many labourers found themselves having to purchase from vendors out of an all too small weekly wage. Gooch reported from Cambridge that at a time when the average winter wage for a labourer was 11s., turf cost 7s. "per 1,000", sedge was 9s. to 12s. "a hundred", and coal was 40s. "per cauldron". In consequence the poor often resorted to using cow dung for fuel. A few years earlier Young had said that the poor in Suffolk had been able to burn "heath and peat" as well as coal[43] but Parkinson, in what is probably the best of the reports on the eastern counties issued by the Board of Agriculture, suggests that enclosure may not only have caused distress, but aggravated it by pushing up the prices of fuel. "As wood is growing scarce [in Huntingdonshire]," he said, "and turf advancing in price, and coals very dear, every possible exertion therefore should be made to find a coalmine, which there is some reason to hope may be discovered in Somersham heath!"[44]

Not only was the English peasant turned into a wage labourer, but, between the years 1790 and 1816, he suffered from the fluctuations in prices brought about by the French wars and rarely, if ever, could have lived far above subsistence level (that is unless he augmented his income or diet by illegal means). Lord Ernle has said that the first sixty-five years of the eighteenth century was the "nearest approach to the Golden Age of the labouring classes" but after that prices began to rise. War was declared in 1793 and thereafter profits and prices rose enormously, the trend being accentuated by an unbelievable succession of bad harvests, shortages, wartime taxation and high interest rates. In the famine year of 1812, wheat was 155s. a quarter compared with the 47s. which was an average for the decade 1785–94.

Wages did not keep pace with prices. There was a definite advance but, to quote Lord Ernle again, it is "certain that, even if wages . . . doubled, the price of provisions . . . trebled. . . . The rise came with startling suddenness and it found him defenceless . . . the labourer had more to buy (because of the loss of his common rights) and what money he had did not go as far as formerly".[45]

Lord Ernle also says that it is exceedingly difficult to arrive at reasonable estimates of the wage increases in this period from the reports to the Board of Agriculture. This is perfectly true, but it is possible to find very comprehensive accounts of income and expenditure for certain districts at different times. These add weight to the generalisations given above.

Arthur Young's survey of Suffolk, for instance (1794, published 1797), gave some very complete figures for day labourers.

Generalising, he said they were paid 1s. 4d. per day with beer in winter, 1s. 6d. in summer and 2s. 10d. a day in harvest. Winter consisted of twenty-nine weeks, summer eighteen weeks and harvest five weeks.[46] At Welnetham the harvesters were paid 12s. a week and were given three bushels of malt. Two years earlier, there had appeared a table of "the necessary expenditure" of a labourer and his wife without family, "communicated by an active magistrate", and calculated at a time when the price of flour was 4s., meal 3s., and allowing £2 10s. 0d. for rent. Expenditure ("not including wear and tear on house and furniture") would be £30 9s. 2d. Income with the wife earning only through gleaning would be £26 0s. 6d.[47]

Young's survey of Essex compared wages in 1803 with those of 1794 and the writer estimated that there had been rises of 53 per cent in the winter and 62 per cent in the summer. He quoted rates for different parishes varying from 10s. to 15s. in winter, and from 11s. to 18s. in summer. He gave no averages for the whole year taking account of harvest wages, although he did say that, at Latchingdon, 2s. 6d. a day was earned during winter and 20s. or 21s. per week in summer. Cottage rents and payments in kind were not given, but the following table of the prices of essentials is informative[48] when compared with his estimate of the percentage by which wages rose. Braintree and Hedingham were the places under discussion.

Price/lb	Butter	Cheese	Mutton	Veal	Beef	Candles	Coal/cauldron
June 1767	6½d.	3¾d.	4½d.	4¼d.	4d.	7¼d.	£1 13s. 0d.
1794	10½d.	6d.	4½d.	5½d.	4½d.		
1805	1/1d.	8d.	7¾d.	9½d.	8d.	11¼d.	£3 0s. 0d.
% rise in 11 years	23¾	33	72	72	77		

Parkinson gave detailed figures of wages earned in Huntingdonshire towards the end of the war. Once again cottage rents are not given but beef at the time was 7½d. per pound, mutton 7d. and veal and lamb 8d. Typical are:

Bythorne—10s. 6d. winter; 12s. summer.
Covington—9s. winter; 10s. summer.
Eyensbury—10s. for eleven months; 11s. one month.
Fenny Stanton—12s. all the year.
Paxton Magna—10s. in winter and £3 10s. 0d. for harvest.
Servant Boy £4; men £12; women £3 10s. 0d. to £5 per annum.

Pidley—12s. milk and small beer in winter; 18s. and small beer in
summer.

Somersham—12s. winter; 15s. summer, and 2 pints of beer; 17s.
per week and meat and drink in harvest.

Staughton—10s. winter; 12s. summer; £3 for harvest.

Thurning—10s. winter; 10s. 6d. summer; harvest £3 13s. 6d. to
£4.

Water Newton—10s. winter; 12s. summer; 15s. in harvest.

Yelling—10s. in winter and 12s. and beer in summer with a
breakfast of bread and milk which they value at about 2d.

Gooch showed very much the same picture in Cambridge at the
same time.[49]

The hours of labour for the rates mentioned above are rarely
quoted. In Huntingdon Parkinson simply recorded them as being
from light until dark in winter, from six to six in the spring and
summer and from light until dark during harvest. Marshall,
sixteen years earlier, after mentioning the difference between
day labourers and yearly servants in Norfolk, summed up the
situation succinctly by saying that "in respect to DAY
LABOURERS, two remarkable circumstances are united; namely
hard work and low wages".[50] Arthur Young in the Essex report
wrote about both long hours and the effect of piece work :[51]

"Hours of labour in summer," he said, "are from six to six; this
begins a little before Lady-Day, and ends a little after Michaelmas.
In part of the interval, from seven to five; and through the re-
mainder from light in the morning till it is dark in the evening."
But, he went on, "the labourers are generally employed by the
piece . . . [and] when the labourer works by the piece, he confines
himself to no particular limits, but in the long summer days, if
vigorous, active and industrious, sometimes continues his application from four in the morning till eight in the evening; and from
his longer continuance, and more vigorous exertion, he not
unfrequently earns one-third more than when he works by the
day. But human nature in general is not capable of this; and the
very strongest constitution it will wear down very fast, and bring
on old age long before its usual period".

The averages given also assume that the labourers were in
continual employment, but it is quite clear that, except during
the summer, many experienced lengthy spells out of work in
East Anglia. Threshing, particularly in the unenclosed parishes,
was practically the only winter employment, and during these

years machines were rapidly being developed to do the work
hitherto done by the flail, thus creating a labour surplus.[52]
These machines, as will be seen later, were particular objects
of hatred, the labourers considering they were a prime cause of
under-employment. In Huntingdon the labourers were apparently employed all winter threshing by hand before their introduction and during the summer would go off to work in better-
paid counties, leaving the farmers with a labour shortage and
reliant upon the "perigrinating Irish".[53]

Marshall's distinction between yearly servants and day
labourers also indicates another way in which many of the
labourers suffered in these years. It had been a common practice
to hire labourers at yearly statute fairs and board them with
the farmer until they left to get married. With the rise of profits
and prices, however, two things happened. It no longer paid to
board servants in husbandry, and the farmer began to regard
himself as someone in a class much higher than that of his
workers. The labourer was turned out of the farmhouse and left
to fend for himself, the old intimacy that once existed, and
which Cobbett in the 'twenties and 'thirties looked nostalgically
back to, was ended for ever. There is plenty of evidence of this
development taking place in East Anglia. Young wrote of it
happening in Norfolk and added in a highly moral tone that it
was "one material cause of an increased neglect of the Sabbath,
and looseness of morals; they [the labourers] are free from the
master's eye, sleep where and with whom they please, and are
rarely seen at church".[54] Sir John Clapham, talking of a Norfolk farmer, said that "He dated the decline [in living in] from
1801, 'when the high price of corn was' (you cease to feed
your men when it is hardest for them to feed themselves). After
that it was discontinued owing to the flourishing state of agriculture during the wars: 'people did not like the trouble of it:
I believe that is the truth.' "[55]

"Formerly a farmer thought it a high luxury if he was able to enjoy
his ale;" said Alexander Baring in a tirade against the high living
of the war years, "but now on entering their houses you were not
only treated with a bottle of port, but sometimes with Madeira.
The sons of these wealthy agriculturists were all fine gentlemen;
instead of following the plough, they were following the hounds,
and the daughters, instead of milking the cows, were using cos-
metics to their hands, that they might look delicate while strum-
ming on the harpsichord."[56]

The practice of living in, however, had by no means completely died out in the eastern districts by the end of the war, and it is surely no coincidence that during the riots *only one* identifiable labourer doing so was on the side of the agitators. In fact, in Ely and Littleport, quite a number who did live in were active in defending the farmers. Gooch, in 1807, described at length the hours worked and the food consumed by some boarders. The contrast between the Spartan fare available to the labourers described as earning 10s. a week and these fortunates is very obvious. They were boarded (for the harvest only it must be admitted) by a gentleman at Wimpole and consumed:

"At six in the morning, one pint of strong beer, and bread and cheese.

"At eight, breakfast of cold meat and beer.

"At eleven, one pint of strong beer and bread and cheese.

"At one, dinner; one day roast beef or mutton, (pork will not do) and plain pudding, next day boiled beef or mutton, and plum-pudding.

"At four, one pint of strong beer, and bread and cheese.

"At seven, hot hash or mutton-pies.

"On Saturday night an addition of good seed-cake of one lb. covered with sugar, and a quart of strong beer poured over it. Hence each man has daily:

"Nine pints of beer (strong);

"Three times bread and cheese;

"Three times meat;

"And on Saturday night, in addition one quart of beer, and a sugared cake. The expense of these will be found great, at the present prices of several articles."

Halévy wrote of the way farmers and labourers had grown apart during the wars—the one class enjoying high profits, learning the art of living well, and the other gradually sinking into depths of untold misery. It was now a purely business relationship between them; it suited the farmer well to have the labourer out of his house, completely reliant upon a weekly wage, and without any distractions like a garden of his own.

What motive, indeed, had the farmer to deal generously? He was a businessman, with his fortune to make—not a fine gentleman for whom the art of good living consisted in knowing how to earn money by toil of others. He would not hear of any useless luxury. He saw no need for the elegant cottages, built pretentiously in

Gothic—as was to be seen on the estates of some great landowners.
A mud hovel, dark and badly ventilated, was quite sufficient. There
must be no field whose cultivation would take up the labourer's
time. A tiny kitchen garden was enough. Every day the labourer
must be at his employer's disposal.[57]

Halévy's description of the cottages of the labourers was true
of the majority, if not all, of those in East Anglia—whether
owned by the farmers or the cottagers themselves. Gooch said
of those in Cambridge that they were "wretchedly bad, speak-
ing generally"[58] and elsewhere that "the poor resident in the
fens resides in miserable huts".[59] "In Suffolk, they [the labourers]
are in generally bad habitations; deficient in all contrivance for
warmth and for convenience. . . ."[60]

George Crabbe described a bedroom in one such dwelling:

> Such is that room which one rude beam divides,
> And naked rafters form the sloping sides;
> Where the vile bands that bind the thatch are seen,
> And lath and mud are all that lie between;
> Save one dull pane, that, coarsely patch'd, gives way
> To the rude tempest, yet excludes the day.[61]

Unhealthy dwellings, low wages, unemployment and the sight
of the wealth and luxury around them which Crabbe said "made
them doubly poor"[62] by no means exhaust the labourers' dismal
catalogue. Added to all these things was a vicious damp climate
over much of the area. The fens, for instance, were liable to
sudden inundations and much of the cultivated land was being
reclaimed by water by 1805, so much so that at Littleport cultivation was said to be "extremely precarious".[63] When the floods
subsided, things were not much better. "The inhabitants of the
Fens are most unhealthy in the season when the Fens are driest,"
reported Gooch, "noxious effects being immediately felt, from the
soil usually under water being exposed to the atmosphere." This
gave rise to the ague, he went on, but conditions had slightly
improved recently as the result of more windmills being erected.[64]
Parkinson described Huntingdon as being "tolerably healthy" in
1811, except in the fenland parts.

These were the conditions the labourers lived under during
the lifetime of the rioters of 1816. It is an appalling list, but the
story is not complete yet. Practically every means of their helping themselves was closed for one reason or another.

CHAPTER TWO

ALTHOUGH EAST ANGLIA is, and always has been, primarily an agricultural area, there were a few industries which offered alternative, or supplementary, employment to many of the labourers and their families. Almost without exception, however, they were declining at the very time they were most needed—during the years when the labourer was already suffering from the ill effects of enclosure and rising prices.

Thomas Stone reported that in Huntingdon there were "no manufactures of note" in 1793 and Parkinson in 1811 practically exhausted his list when he had mentioned the making of Kimbolton lace, a paper mill at St. Neots and two sacking factories at Standground. Another correspondent, however, wrote:

There are no manufactures carried on in the county, except the brewery (and that not for exportation), together with a little woolstapling, but the women and children (at least such of them as are able to work), may have constant employment in spinning yarn, which is put out by the generality of the country shopkeepers, though at present it is but a very indifferent means of employment and they always prefer out of doors work when the season comes on.[1]

The woollen industry had long been an important source of employment in Eastern England, but during the war it declined rapidly as the centres of production moved elsewhere. Weavers and spinners began to experience distress as bad as the agricultural labourers and conditions grew worse with the cessation of war orders. It is impossible to determine how many were among the rioters of 1816, but the Duke of Grafton (the Lord Lieutenant of Suffolk) writing to Sidmouth in April 1816 described the riots and dreadful suffering in Cosford Hundred as caused "through the total failure of the spinning of long wool, which used to afford employment to so many thousand persons in this county", an opinion which was endorsed by the magistrates meeting at Bury St. Edmunds shortly afterwards,[2] where spinning jennies were broken in May.

Plenty of evidence is available of distress in the woollen indus-

try in the twenty or thirty years prior to 1816 although it is
clear that the decline in the trade affected certain processes and
skills more than others. The spinners, for instance, suffered earlier than the weavers.[3] Arthur Young, writing in 1807,[4] said that
"the average earnings" of the best spinners at Dunmow (Essex)
was "scarcely 4d. a day; 40 years ago commonly 8d.". Elsewhere
he said that "the woollen manufacture for time immemorial has
taken the lead in this county; but from its long continued dwind-
ling condition, it is uncertain whether it will many years remain
so".[5] The manufacture of baize was ruined at places like Dunmow and Colchester which relied largely on export orders for
Spain.[6] Norwich was the very heart of the industry, but there
things were no better. "A few years ago the trade gave employment to more than five hundred combers, and furnished spinning
for most of the women and children of this, and the adjoining
county," it was reported in 1810. "But the machines, which
have long been used in Yorkshire for preparing yarn, have
been lately introduced here, whereby the process of manual
combing and spinning are nearly superseded."[7] William George
Carter, secretary of the Association for the Relief of the Manufacturing Poor, asked about the decline of Halstead, where 2,012
out of a population of 3,279 were then in receipt of poor relief,
said it was because "a former woollen manufactory was established there, which has now ceased".[8] Bocking, although it had
"not entirely ceased to be a manufacturing parish", had
"declined considerably for the last twenty years. . . . It [had]
become agricultural, with a burden of manufacturing poor on
it".[9] Frederick Schoberl, writing in 1813, described a number
of Suffolk villages, some of which became prominent as centres
of the riots in 1816, in like manner. For instance:

The woollen manufacture, which was once very flourishing in this
town [Neyland], is reduced to a low ebb, only some yarn being
made for the manufacture of crape and bombazeen at Norwich.
Bildeston was described as "a small town, meanly built . . . It was
once noted for its manufacture of bluecloth and blankets, which
are now dwindled away to the spinning of yarn".

Of these manufactures [connected with the woollen industry] Lavenham now has nothing but the spinning of woollen yarn, and the
making of calimancoes. A considerable manufacture of hempen
cloth has, however, of late years, been established in this town.[10]

The various trades and skills connected with the growing and
processing of hemp had also helped the labourers with additional
work, but these, too, were declining. This is shown in the number of "Hicklers" (or "Hitchelors"), weavers, and others connected
with the trade who appear in local records, applying for relief
under the Poor Law and Settlement Acts.[11] Only Mark Benton,
a sixty-year-old, among those committed to the Special Assizes
at Ely made any money from growing hemp, yet at places like
Outwell it had been a major crop under the open-field system.[12]
Even as late as 1804 Arthur Young had said that, in the Downham area, hemp was grown in large quantities by the cottagers.[13]
In another of his reports he described the organisation of the
trade. The hemp was harvested, then bought by women who
would

"spin it into yarn which they carry to market, and sell at prices
proportionate to the fineness. The spinners earn better and more
steady wages than by wool" . . . he went on in words that were not
applicable some fifteen years later. "Nor is the trade, like wool, subject to great depressions, there being always more work than hands;
the consequence of a brisk demand. They begin to spin at four or
five years old : it is not so difficult to spin hemp as wool . . ."[14]

With local industry dying, the labourers might have been
expected to have migrated to the industrial areas, but they were
often prevented from doing this by the Settlement Laws. These
were of seventeenth-century origin and were passed because
"poor people are not restrained from going from one parish to
another, and therefore do endeavour to settle themselves in those
parishes where there is the best stock, the largest commons or
wastes to build cottages, and the most woods for them to burn
and destroy; and when they have consumed it, then to another
parish; and at last become rogues and vagabonds".[15] By 1816
these had become onerous and out of date, often denying the
labourer the right to seek higher wages elsewhere and constitut-
ing, according to the Hammonds, a "capricious tyranny".

There are disagreements about the extent to which the Settlement Laws were actually used during the eighteenth and nineteenth centuries, it being pointed out, for instance, that the great
northern cities grew up despite them. What is certain, however,
is that tremendous hardship and injustice was suffered by individuals and that the labourers considered the Laws intolerable.
Furthermore, they must have contributed to the rooting of a

"slothful" and uneducated populace to their places of birth and so directly contributed to the creation of the mass of discontented surplus labour that existed throughout the agrarian districts in 1816.[16]

The Settlement Laws, as they stood in 1816, provided that a person could qualify for poor relief only in the parish in which he or she had a settlement. This could be gained in a number of ways and employers and parish officials resorted to every possible means to stop a person becoming chargeable. For instance, a farmer described to the Select Committee on the Poor Laws in 1817 how he and his colleagues got round the provision whereby a labourer having been hired for a year could obtain a settlement.[17] After saying that if residence alone gave labourers a settlement he would "pull down the[ir] cottages", he went on,

we hire men in our own parish by the year, but never out of the parish; the only sure way to prevent a young man gaining a settlement in your parish, which I can devise, is to hire him for a fixed time short of a year, by which means we avoid the implication of yearly hiring; if we do not hire them absolutely for a short period with a service for a year, hiring is presumed, therefore we limit the time.[18]

Until 1795, to prevent the arbitrary eviction of newcomers to a parish, some authorities had granted labourers certificates acknowledging liability for them if they became paupers. In that year Pitt was responsible for the passing of an Act which abolished certificates and established the principle that a labourer could not be forcibly removed until he became actually chargeable, and then at the removing parish's expense. This left plenty of room for quarrels between authorities, however, and the sums spent on removing paupers and on litigation between parishes were enormous. The poor of Snettisham at the turn of the century must have felt "doubly poor" if they read that "Expenditure in suits of law, removal of paupers, and expenses of overseers and other officers . . . amounts to £6,031 17s. 9¾d. (1801)".[19] In Cambridge it was reckoned that "Between 1662 and 1834 two-thirds of the time of the County Bench must, on an average, have been occupied with appeals touching this matter; two-thirds of existing parochial papers are concerned with the movement of pauper pawns across the chessboard of Cambridgeshire".[20] William Rankin, of Bocking, asked about removals, said that "we find it a very heavy expense; our legal expenses, and the expenses of litigation on removals, is very heavy". One family, he went on, was carried to Norwich, a distance of seventy miles.[21] Out of seven cases reported from the Quarter Sessions at Huntingdon in January 1816 in *The Cambridge Chronicle,* four were concerned with disputes over the removal of paupers.[22] This is typical of the whole period, over the whole of the area.

The causes of litigation under the Settlement Laws were endless, and evidence of the complexity of the issues involved can be found in the *Report from the Select Committee on the Poor Laws, 1817.* Huge sums were spent in attempts to save the small sums for which the paupers would have qualified.

There were serious attempts to legislate to improve the labourer's lot between 1790 and 1816, but all were unsuccessful. Parliament was unprepared to help him, but members of the aristocracy were quite free with advice to the labourer on how to economise and make do at the time of his greatest distress. The Hammonds give numerous examples, and dismal reading they make. They are illustrative of a prevailing attitude of mind and show how completely out of sympathy one class[23] was with another. Suggestions that they substitute oatmeal bread for the wheaten loaf must have seemed a final humiliation to labourers eating little else.[24] Equally ridiculous must have appeared some of the attempts to alleviate distress by private philanthropy at a national level. The London Association for the Relief of the Labouring and Manufacturing Poor, a noisy body that attracted considerable attention in 1816,[25] had a scheme, for instance, "to increase the supply of Fish for the tables of the wealthy, diminishing the necessity for the usual quantity of meat, and thus reducing its price to the inferior orders of society".[26] Large quantities of fish were bought and arrangements made to transport it inland, but with what success is not known.

Suffering from the effects of inflation, long periods of unemployment, the decline of domestic industry, and often denied the right to seek work elsewhere, the labourer often had no other choice but to resort to the parish and seek relief. The Poor Law, as it existed in England before 1834, had its origin in Elizabethan times. The parish constituted the unit and the system was administered by overseers of the poor, to whom paupers had to apply. Funds were obtained by the levying of a poor rate.

The method of giving relief varied, but was usually one of two kinds : out relief, which consisted of giving the poor a weekly dole at home, and indoor relief, given in a workhouse or house of industry. Early in the eighteenth century a great impetus was given to the building of these places by an Act which enabled overseers, with the consent of the vestry, to set up parish work-houses or farm out the poor. These places were often loathsome enough, but they were of supreme importance to the labourer who had to resort to them during bad times. Towards the end of the eighteenth century, however, in many parts of East Anglia these were supplanted when local Acts of Parliament were obtained by which Houses of Industry were set up for a number of parishes or Incorporations. In these, control was exercised by a number of "Directors of the Poor" and salaried officials who had enormous authority and were, by general consent, harsher in their attitudes than had been the J.P.s and those responsible for the parish houses.[27] Between 1760 and 1785 "over the greater part [of Norfolk and Suffolk] the administration of the Poor Law [was] withdrawn from the parish officers and vested in fourteen new bodies of Incorporated Guardians of the Poor".[28]

The labourers loathed the parish overseers, but hated the guardians of the incorporations even more. By the same mental process that led them to glamorise the unenclosed village they convinced themselves that they were being deprived of their liberties, and in Suffolk there were serious riots against the union houses that spread over thirty years. The one at Bulcamp, for instance, known as "Bulcamp Hell", was destroyed and £500 worth of damage done. Ten days earlier the Nacton house, which catered for forty-six parishes in the Hundreds of Colnies and Carlford, had been attacked by a mob of four hundred labourers who had said they had come "to fight for their liber-ties" and were "resolved the poor should be maintained in their own parishes".[29]

In most of the large Suffolk workhouses the inmates were employed in washing, spinning and combing wool. In a few of them agricultural work was done on land attached to the house and at Nacton, as well as spinning, the paupers made cordage, sacking and plough lines. At Downham where "the poor [were] partly farmed" the contractor received £95 a year for maintaining twenty in a house, and 2s. a head for each one above that number. They were employed spinning jersey or worsted and the contractor, of course, kept their earn-ings. When Eden wrote (June 1795), there were "26 inmates, viz., 7 under 9 years, 4 from 9 to 20, the rest from 25 to 70". There were, he concluded, "4 bastards and 3 soldiers' wives".[30]

Many of the workhouses, whether run by the parish or an incorporation, were disease-ridden, and, of course, the worst of them became equated with the norm in popular imagination. Epidemics were common occurrences. Arthur Young mentioned smallpox, measles, whooping cough and "fever" as regular visitors in the county of Suffolk, and, in 1781, during one outbreak, the infamous house at Bulcamp lost 130 inhabitants.[31] At an institution in Norfolk in 1764 half the inmates were killed by disease, and twenty-four years later child deaths in the same place were one in eight.[32] This was largely the result of overcrowding. J. C. Curwen, M.P., in a speech in the House of Commons in May 1816 referred to workhouses as "mansions of misery", and, he went on, "To such a shameless a pitch has it now arisen that pauperism is contemplated and calculated on in the very outset of life".[33]

Added to the miseries of hard work, overcrowding and disease was often a rigid and cruel discipline. A description of Bulcamp given to some government officials said that control of the incorporation was "vested in twenty-four directors and twenty-four guardians. The directors are landed proprietors and magistrates; and are elected for life; the guardians are elected periodically, and the qualification for the office is being assessed at not less than 60L". The inmates were dressed in the uniform of the incorporation and the "disobedient and refractory" were "punished by order of the Committee, by solitary confinement or a diminution of diet . . .".[34] The rules of the house at Melton included statements that, "All paupers, whether in the house or receiving quarterly allowances to wear a badge P.L.W."; "No allowance to be granted to any person who keeps a dog, except a shepherd or warrender"; "It is provided that no child should be apprenticed who has not had smallpox".[35]

Any number of descriptions of the indignities suffered by the poor in the workhouses can be found. Probably the most famous is contained in Crabbe's poem *The Village*. It makes an interesting comparison with the more sober and detached observations on houses of industry by the Reverend George Howlett, one "of the ablest and best informed pamphleteers of that generation". Crabbe wrote that:

> Theirs is yon house that holds the parish-poor,
> Whose walls of mud scarce bear the broken door;
> There, where the putrid vapours, flagging, play,
> And the dull wheel hums doleful through the day;—

> There children dwell who know no parent's care;
> Parents, who know no children's love, dwell there!
> Heart-broken matrons on their joyless bed,
> Forsaken wives, and mothers never wed;
> Dejected widows with unheeded tears,
> And crippled age with more than childhood fears;
> The lame, the blind, and, far the happiest they!
> The moping idiot and the madman gay.[36]

Howlett told Arthur Young that:

After a pretty full and minute investigation of the subject of houses of industry, I have not been able to discover any useful tendency in them, but in two respects; first, the general aversion of the poor from entering those houses, as it were, compels them to do their utmost, and even to submit to great hardships, rather than apply for parochial relief; and, secondly, that the business being in some measure to a point by means of them, is more easily transacted.[37]

Pressure on workhouse accommodation and increased distress resulting from wartime price increases caused magistrates in many parts of the country to adopt a scheme of poor relief, tried, first of all, in Berkshire. This was the so-called Speenhamland "system", that, whatever its original intention was, succeeded in demoralising the poor even further. It was a system in line with the practices of the past, an exception to the generalisation about the move away from "paternalism" mentioned earlier.

The magistrates of Berkshire took their momentous decisions at a meeting at the *Pelican Inn*, Speenhamland, in May 1795. The idea of a fixed legal minimum wage was rejected as being inexpedient and farmers were asked to raise wages; whether they did so or not, however, it was decided that the labourer was to get a subsistence wage brought up to an agreed level, if necessary, by a supplement from the parish. The J.P.s drew up a scale of wages tied to the price of bread and their example spread like wildfire. Variations, of course, there were, but over the whole of East Anglia the Speenhamland system was adopted in one form or another. In Cambridgeshire, for instance, scales were common throughout the whole county by 1800.[38]

The effects of the new system of poor relief were disastrous. It was immaterial to a labourer living in a district where the scheme had been adopted whether he worked or not—his meagre income was assured anyway. Within a few years he began to look upon his allowance as a right, and this could well be one of the major reasons for his lack of antagonism to authority in the years of dreadful suffering. He had a vested interest in maintaining things as they were—fearing that any change might (as his experience surely had taught him) be one for the worse. The Poor Law which had once been intended as "a hospital" had become "a prison" for the poor. Why should he try to break out? He was completely demoralised and only the heaping of additional burdens on him in the early part of 1816 caused him to stir, and then ineffectively. Contemporary writers recognised the extent of his demoralisation and Speenhamland did not lack its critics (although, as often as not, they had no practical alternatives to suggest).

Young reported as early as 1797 that in Suffolk

That relief which formerly was and still ought to be petitioned for as a favour, is now frequently demanded as a right; that idleness and intemperance which formerly feared to be observed, now obtrusively presses forward to sight; the pauper is no longer satisfied with his allowance, nor the labourer with his hire . . .[39]

The Rev. Glover, Rector of South Repps and Vicar of Cromer (Norfolk), said twenty years later that the poor relief system had given rise to

"the degraded and discontented character of our poor" and "divided us into two classes, not of rich and poor . . . but into paupers and receivers of parochial aid; which have divested pauperism of all shame and all disgrace, and led the poor to look upon the parish as a ready and always available substitute for their own exertions . . . and taught fraud and importunity to supply the place of that energy of mind and body, which could once animate them to search and to find employment in one direction when it had failed in another . . ."[40]

". . . that general degradation which has taken place in the moral habits and feeling of the lower orders of society", concerned W. Peter in an article in The Pamphleteer in 1816. "To accept parochial charity was formerly a disgrace," he went on, "it is now demanded as a privilege."[41]

Extracts from the Report from the Select Committee on Labourers Wages (1824) show that Mr. Peter's remarks were applicable to Eastern England. "In parts of . . . Norfolk a labourer is quite certain of obtaining an allowance from the parish, sufficient to support his family; it consequently becomes a matter of indifference to him

whether he earns a small sum or a large one."[42] ". . . on this allowance, whether idle or industrious, the labourer relies as a right;
and when he receives less, he makes an angry appeal to a Magistrate,
not as a petitioner for charity, but as a claimant for justice."[43] Suffolk
was described as one of the counties where "the plan of paying
wages out of the poor rate, has been carried to the greatest extent".[44] The Rev. Anthony Collett described its effect on the poor
in Blything Hundred, where the house at Bulcamp was situated,
by saying "It has totally demoralised the lower orders; it has made
them poachers, thieves and robbers . . ."[45] A pamphlet signed by
Richard Whateley called the Poor Law system in Suffolk "a bounty
on idleness . . . a bounty on theft".[46]

"When Mr. Rodwell, who is the present occupier of this parish
[Little Liversmere] came into possession," a later parliamentary
committee was told, "he sent for the labourers for the purpose of
coming to terms with them; but they declared it was immaterial
to them what wages he allowed, as they would be made up by the
statement. He, however, gave them to understand, that he would
not deal with them in that way, and offered them such wages as
he considered just, and promised to keep them, their wives and
children, in constant employment. This caused great dissatisfaction
for some time and there were constant threats held out against
him, and appeals made to the Magistrates . . ."[47]

Just as the labourer had little to gain from working con-
scientiously, or from working at all, so the farmer had little
incentive to employ him full time. The old contacts between
farmers and labourers were breaking down already as the result
of social and economic pressures, and the inevitable antagonisms
growing up between employer and wage labourer. This antagonism must have been sharpened by the way in which the farmers
—or at least the larger ones—were able to use the Poor Law to
their own advantage.

A number of methods of public employment for paupers had
grown up and been adopted by the various types of Poor Law
Authorities. Direct employment by the parish was one; and the
labour rate system, under which paupers were shared out among
ratepayers, was another; a third was the "roundsman system"
in which labour was sold to farmers by the Authority, naturally
at a wage lower than the prevailing rate. By these last means it
was hoped to keep the amounts spent on poor relief down, and
it may have done so. But it also became extremely easy for
farmers who had been employing labourers full time to dismiss

them, force them on to the parish and take on workers subsidised by the Authority. By this means larger farmers could make their smaller neighbours contribute to their wage bills via the rates. "After 1815, the number of permanent servants on the farm was brought as low as possible. The operations of agriculture were carried on by a skeleton staff, which was reinforced when necessary by a body of labourers taken off the parish for some weeks and put back there as soon as they had completed their work."[48] The labourers resented the manipulating of the Poor Law intensely. When the rioters at Ely forced the magistrates to agree to their demands and formulate them and publicise them, one of the major concessions was that "the labourer shall be paid his full wages by the Farmer who Hires him". A magistrate described the system as it worked in and around Woodbridge,

In my, and many other, parishes, the farmers employ all that want work, paying supernumeraries less than the wages of regular or constant men. . . . . In other parishes farmers take a certain number of these supernumeraries, on the requisition of the overseer, according to the rating of the farmer, perhaps one for every 40, 30 or 20 pounds, and for each man 6s. a week for his work. If the labourer has a family, he receives sufficient out of the poor rates to maintain them, and in the following proportion :— for his wife only, about 1s.; if one child, 2s.; two children, 3s. 6d.; three children, 5s 6d.; four children, 6s. 6d.; and so on . . .[49]

The policy of Poor Law officials, representing the employers and rate payers, was, of course, to keep relief as low as possible.

Sometimes, too, especially in districts with a "surplus" population, either the relief given or the rate of wages was so low that the total income merely sufficed to sustain life.

The principal calculation of the overseer is the amount of what will merely support existence.[50]

It is not surprising that labourers, unable to obtain more food than would "merely support existence", resorted increasingly to crime. Poaching had never been regarded by them as morally wrong and in the early years of the nineteenth century the pickings from an incursion into the preserves increased enormously. Improvements had been made in the design and manufacture of sporting rifles, and the rearing, preserving and shooting of game had become the main relaxation of country society. Numerous associations for the preserving of game sprang up,[51] based on the aforementioned voluntary organisations for the prosecution of felons, and the labourers retaliated by organising themselves into gangs. In some areas there existed what amounted to a full scale poaching war and the press of the time contains hundreds of accounts of pitched battles at night that ended in imprisonment, transportation and often executions. John Orridge, who was Governor of both the gaol and the House of Correction in Bury St. Edmunds,[52] told a Select Committee that, in his area, however, the dramatic increase in poaching crimes coincided "with the laying down of fox hounds".[53]

The poaching war did as much as anything else in the early nineteenth century to widen the gulf between the classes in rural England. On the one hand were the landowners employing gamekeepers[54] and organised in associations,[55] which quite openly appealed—with very little success—for informers, and on the other the gangs. There can be no doubt that, in an inarticulate way, the labourers regarded their nightly activities as some form of class war. Francis Pym, a magistrate of Longstowe, Cambridgeshire, asked whether he thought the labourers regarded poaching as a crime, replied, "No, I think not; they do not consider [it] to be a moral offence."[56]

Denied adequate relief, deprived of alternative employment, forced to steal, discouraged from working at home and unable to go elsewhere, the labourer's lot might have seemed at the lowest ebb possible in the latter years of the French wars. Between Waterloo and May 1816, however, when riots eventually broke out in East Anglia, conditions actually got worse. It was in those few months that the final indignities which led to violence were heaped upon the labourers.

CHAPTER THREE

"TILL 1813 THE war and the continental system had kept up prices," wrote Halévy, "but with the fall of Napoleon fell the ring fence of English agriculture."[1] Farmers and landowners had grown accustomed to the high rents, high profits and high living of the war years, and, when they discovered that these were coming to an end, took part in terrific campaigns to safeguard themselves. Shortly after the conclusion of one particularly noisy campaign in 1816, the labourers' riots broke out in East Anglia. Too much must not be made of this, but there is some evidence to suggest that the labourers took note of their masters resisting authority and drew the obvious inferences. Certainly the behaviour of "the superior orders" in rural England in 1816 was no credit to them. Byron described them as "The first to make a malady of the peace".

> The peace has made one general malcontent
> Of these high-market patriots; war was rent![2]

The harvest of 1813 was an exceptionally good one, and there was an abundance which had not been used up at the time of the harvest of the following year. A fall in prices ensued which was aggravated by the opening of the continental markets later. The price of a quarter of wheat was 112s. in the summer, but by December 1814 was down to 75s. 6d. By January the price was 52s. 6d.

Falling prices mean relative prosperity for the labourer, assuming he is in regular employment at a steady rate of pay. There is reliable evidence, however, that farmers in East Anglia reduced wages at this time (and of course Speenhamland was an added inducement to do so).[3] Examples of wage rates for earlier periods have been quoted at some length, and they make an interesting comparison with the earnings of prisoners fully committed for trial for offences during the riots at Ely and Littleport. Weekly earnings varied, according to a list prepared for the Treasury Solicitor, from 4s. to £1, but most people received amounts varying from 6s. to 15s. The list will be included as an appendix, and it is a very comprehensive document indeed, giving details of the size of family, parish allowances, ownership of cottages, gardens, allotments and so on. William Dann, for instance, had five children, earned 15s. and had a weekly allowance of 2s.; Isaac Harley, a labourer, had two children, earned 9s. and got nothing from the parish; Henry Mainer, James Newell and Robert Porter, single labourers, earned 6s., 8s., and 9s. respectively; James Wortley, a married man from Littleport, had four children, earned 8s. and was allowed 1s. 3d.[4] Some were unemployed; many were obviously underemployed.

The labourers were not unused to winter unemployment, but, in the aftermath of the war, farmers sacked their workers at a time of the year when work was normally plentiful. The Board of Agriculture showed this in a volume called *The Agricultural State of the Kingdom*, published in the summer of 1816, which gives a most comprehensive picture of rural England in the months before the labourers' revolt. It was based on replies to a circular sent to leading farmers and landowners which included the question, "What is the State of the Labouring Poor; and what is the Proportion of Poor Rates, compared with the years 1811 and 1812?". There were 273 replies of which 237 denoted "a want of employment, in terms more or less forcible". Of these, 101 "expatiating on the degree of this want of employment, describe the extreme distress resulting from it as amounting to great misery and wretchedness, and in some cases, to an alarming degree". Twenty-five replies were favourable and eighteen said conditions were neither better nor worse than they had been for many years, but a note in the preface said that these places were expected to be as bad as elsewhere by the time of publication.[5] Replies from the East Anglian counties were very full. J. Wing, writing about a part of Cambridgeshire, said that:

The State of the labouring poor is very deplorable, and arises entirely from the want of employment, which they are willing to seek, but the farmer cannot afford to furnish. The poor ... say, they never experienced such bad times. A parish in the next county, (without any manufacture) consisting of 3,500 acres, has, at this time 72 men, besides boys, out of employment, and upon the parish; the poor-rates are increasing, in an unexampled and alarming degree, in all other places.[6]

The Rev. Thomas Fenton described conditions in his part of Suffolk: "the labouring poor are in as bad a situation as they were in the dear years. One third of them being out of employment, and their wages being reduced by more than another third, and the prices of every article of their consumption (bread excepted) being nearly equal to the prices of the years 1811 and 1812."[7]

Thomas Archer also wrote of a part of Suffolk. "At the present moment we have two parishes, *Mildenhall and Isleham,* which, together have very few, if any, short of 100 labourers, and most of them very hearty young men, for whom the farmers cannot find regular work. These men are driven to apply to the parish officers for relief for the support of themselves and families."[8]

At Lavenham, "The state of the industrious labouring poor" was described as "very distressing (mere paupers I take not into the account, for they are not much affected by any change in the times), those I mean who have formerly been accustomed to support themselves and a small family in plenty and comfort : these, from the very great scarcity of labour, are forced to go off with half their former earnings, which are reluctantly made up from the parish fund in the same proportion with the pay of other paupers. These are certainly real objects of pity, and one cannot help feeling for the severity of their lot".[9]

Another clergyman said that in his area "The state of the Labouring Poor is very bad, compared with what it was four or five years ago. They can get but little employment now (1816) and instead of 2s. 6d. per day as it was at the time stated, they *now* have only 1s. 6d. per day".[10]

Robert Marsham reported "Great want of work . . . stout, able hands engage to work at eightpence per day, by the *Overseers,* consequently the rates higher than in 1811 . . ."[11]

The replies were tabulated. Those for Norfolk included :

> "Worse than in the dearest times."
> "Distressed from want of employment."
> "Very bad; 15s. per week reduced to 9s."
> "Truly distressing; many unemployed."
> "Want employment."
> "A great many quite out of employment."
> "1—4th out of employment."
> "Much distressed; 1—3rd or 1—4th unemployed."
> "Fewer employed—poor houses crowded."
> "Employed, but many by Parish officers."

Labourers who had never been out of work before were thrown on to the Parish and into the workhouses in the early months of 1816. In the Hundreds of Mutford and Lothingland,

admissions into the house of industry were the highest ever
known and the authorities were forced to allow out-relief, while
wages for those in work were said to be 1s. 4d. to 1s. 6d. a day.
John Thurtell reported that on "Monday, the 12th inst. (February 1816) the applications for relief amounted to 150, and on
Monday, the 19th, to 175".[12] The "House of Industry for the
Incorporated Hundreds of Loddon and Clavering . . . [was] completely full, having no less than 400 paupers; and on Monday,
the 19th, 150 labourers (all stout, active men, willing but unable
to procure work) applied to be relieved".[13]

Labourers relieved outside the workhouses were often employed on parish work in large numbers. Throwing aggrieved
people together was liable to engender an ugly attitude, particularly when news of riots in other parts of the country filtered
into the villages, and when prices began to rise again in April.[14]
Correspondents writing to the Board of Agriculture from the
eastern counties noted it happening. Robert Fuller said that the
"Labourers have nothing to do; and I consider, *and am sure,* that
if the poor laws are not revised very soon, that the country cannot be at peace long; for if the labouring hands are out of employ, they will assemble together, and lay plans to deceive the
magistrates, the churchwardens, and overseers, which is daily the
case here".[15] John Thompson, writing from Suffolk, devoted the
whole of his reply to the insurrectionary attitude which, he said,
was developing there.

One of the most alarming symptoms of a decline is the situation of
the labouring poor; numbers are out of employ, because their
masters cannot pay them for work. What then is to be done? They
cannot starve! They are sent to work in the roads, and are maintained by the poor-rate. Thus the evil day (payment) is postponed
to some future time! I was informed last week, by two gentlemen
who saw them, that they passed by a gravel pit where forty persons of this description should have been at work; on the contrary,
some were ringing a peal on their shovels—some, acting as serjeants,
drilling their men, &c., &c. Dreadful symptoms of a decline; and if
some immediate relief cannot be obtained, I may conclude by saying, "On the verge, nay even in the gulph of bankruptcy".[16]

Increased pauperism and unemployment led to an increase
in poaching crimes which hardened class attitudes even further.
This is mentioned again and again by witnesses before the Select
Committee on Criminal Commitments.

During the very months when conditions were worsening in rural England, Parliament was debating an Act to alter the penalties for poaching. These had been increased in 1800 and the maximum penalty then laid down was one month's hard labour in a House of Correction. Sixteen years later the maximum was put up again to a punishment of seven years' transportation. The consequence was not a dropping off in the crime rate, but more violent resistance to arrest by the poachers.[17] At Downham Market, one of the major trouble centres later, the local gentry hired a Bow Street officer for four months. He masqueraded as a gentleman's servant, gained the poachers' confidence and became their salesman. He then laid information against them and they were prosecuted.[18] One of the avowed aims of the Downham rioters in May was to liberate the poachers.[19]

While Parliament was increasing the penalties for poaching, and the labourers being thrown on to the parish, farmers and landowners were engaged at a local level in rowdy campaigns to better their own positions—always claiming, of course, that they were acting in the interests of the agricultural community as a whole.[20] As soon as conditions worsened with the opening of continental markets, demands for protection went up. Pitt had been responsible for an Act passed in 1804 by which the price above which corn was permitted to enter the country duty free was fixed at 66s. This had never come into effect, but, when prices began to fall in 1813, an agitation, both noisy and successful, was begun to get the level raised. After a rebuff in 1814,[21] an incredibly unpopular Act was passed the following year prohibiting free entry under 80s. Harriet Martineau put a view of the landed interest's behaviour as it appeared to contemporaries.

When they demanded that foreign corn should be no longer warehoused duty free, it was manifest that they utterly set at naught every possible precaution against a season of dearth. Their relief was to be attained at all hazards by the most absolute and unconditional monopoly. The bonded corn could not be let out of the warehouse till the home price had reached 80s. . . .[22]

"One thing seems certain :" wrote W. Smart, "that the country, apart from the landowning class, was dead against the bill. As one speaker said, never had their wishes been so generally and so unequivocally expressed. This indeed was scarcely denied, the only answers attempted being that the petitioners [against the bills]—

the 'lower orders' as they were abundantly called—did not understand what they were signing, or what was good for them. 'The
people might as well petition for the abolition of their liberties as
for the abandonment of the measure' said [Charles]Western."[23]

The selfish campaign for protection must have impressed the
labourers, but even more striking was the fight against the property tax. Heady language, mass meetings and violence produced results. The tax had originally been imposed as a wartime
measure only. Parliament was prorogued from July 1815 to
February 1816 and, when it met, Castlereagh asked for the im-
post to be continued. Immediately a campaign was started in the
City of London which Henry Brougham and Alexander Baring
took over. Nationwide meetings were held and eventually
"Above six weeks were almost entirely spent by the House of
Commons in receiving the numberless petitions poured in from
all quarters against the tax".[24]

The Eastern counties were prominent in the campaign. Practically every issue of the local Press during 1815 and the early
months of 1816 contains accounts of huge meetings ending in
a decision to petition Parliament. One at Stowmarket attended
by 4,000 people in February 1815, for instance, asked for protection and the repeal of the income tax, and another in March
of the following year wanted the Government "to take into consideration the distressed state of the agricultural interest in the
county" and asked for "relief from the Income Tax and the
war tax upon malt".[25] In March 1816, *The Bury and Norwich
Post* said that "The 'Income Tax' still continues to be the ex-
clusive subject of attention",[26] while one of the Cambridge
papers, in the same month, quite truthfully said it was "mono-
polising public interest". Mr. Gooch, one of the most prominent
of the representatives from the agricultural areas, presented a
petition against the tax from 1,000 people in Suffolk to the Commons in February, and petitions from Norfolk flowed in regularly, calling it "unjust, unequal and inquisitional".[27]

The campaign in East Anglia was not always free from violence. As early as December 1814 there was trouble in Huntingdonshire. The populace in the St. Ives area were notified of "a
considerable advance in the usual assessment on property" and
then proceeded to hold a meeting at the *Crown Inn* where, it
was reported,

more than three hundred persons assembled, who, rushing themselves into the Commissioners' room, seized the Inspector, and
forced him out through the glass window into the yard, by which
he was considerably cut and bruised. The tumult increased so much
without side, that the officer only effected his escape from this
popular resentment by privately passing through several neighbouring houses; the people then proceeded to the Inspector's house, the
windows of which they instantly destroyed. The Commissioners, we
understand, at length appeased their fury, by a declaration that no
rise of the tax should take place for the present.[28]

The St. Ives incident was not an isolated one. The Huntingdonshire correspondent of *The Cambridge Gazette* drew attention to an advertisement that appeared in the public notices
columns of his journal. It was headed "Public Confession" and
referred to an incident in an area which became a trouble spot
in 1816.

"We, the undersigned," it read, "occupiers of lands in Upwell, Outwell, Welney and Denver did riotously assemble together on 31st
December 1814 and obstruct the Commissioners executing the
Property Tax for the said Division at Downham that day . . . for
which offence His Majesty's Attorney General hath filed his information against us in the Court of King's Bench . . . we are (because
the tax has been collected since) more strongly convinced of the
gross impropriety and illegality of our conduct."[29]

The nine signatories ended by asking for the case to be dropped and offering to pay all expenses.

It is not known what happened to the Norfolk rioters but at
the Huntingdon Assizes in March 1816 Joseph Thorpe and
others (held over from the Summer Assizes) were charged "for a
riot and obstruction of the Commissioners executing the Property
Act" at St. Ives.[30] The prisoners all expressed their contrition
and after a rebuke from the Judge proceedings were dropped.
For hardly more serious riots labourers were executed, transported
and imprisoned in great numbers, a few months later. Nobody
at the time referred to the fact that they were in some ways
merely copying the behaviour of their masters a short time
before.

The same issues of the newspapers that reported Thorpe's
acquittal reported the ending of the Property Tax. The campaign
led by Brougham and Baring had finally been successful and

the victory was hailed with tremendous enthusiasm. Resistance to Government was celebrated throughout the country in a way more appropriate for the ending of a war. *The Times*, which had been very strongly against the tax, announced its abolition and wished "forever sunk in the catalogue of words be that detestable compound! Perish, if possible, the recollection of its meaning from the mind of freemen".[31] *The Courier*, a ministerial newspaper which persisted in regarding the tax as "the best means of raising so large a sum with little or no pressure upon the poorer classes of people", said that its repeal showed quite conclusively that the House of Commons spoke "the sense of the people of England",[32] an observation which could have been construed as an encouragement to would-be demonstrators. In Cambridge the "Momentous Victory" and the "triumph of public good taste" was welcomed with bellringing,[33] while in Swaffham the inhabitants were reported to be considering taking down the flags put up on the church to mark the end of the war and replacing them with "a device and inscription" containing the names of the thirty-seven independent M.P.s whose votes made repeal possible—"to hand to posterity the glorious defeat . . . over that war monster the Property Tax".[34]

All these campaigns were accompanied by an enormous amount of publicity, so much that "Hapless indeed would be the situation of the members of our Cabinet", wrote the editor of one journal, "were they to wade through all the literary productions that are addressed to them".[35] Charles Western's pamphlet containing the speech and the resolutions he proposed in the House of Commons was only the most famous and widely noticed[36] of them. All admitted that the lot of the labourers was deplorable. (Western, for instance, said that they were "at the present moment suffering under the pressure of unexampled distress".) This was usually put down to a bad system of poor relief, but it is interesting to note what the spokesmen of the farming interest regarded as the cause of their *own* troubles.

The questionnaire circulated by the Board of Agriculture in February asked for opinions about the cause of the depression. High rents,[37] the Property Tax and the Malt Tax (repealed together) were universally referred to in the replies, but the tithe was only occasionally mentioned. Western said that he considered the crisis was the result of the "surplus produce" left over from the year before. Some writers thought that the restrictions on cash payments were the basic cause of the trouble, an opinion shared by Cobbett and Brougham.

Cobbett was a well-known opponent of paper currency. The sudden increase in the price of corn just before the riots in May, which made matters even worse for the labourers, was, according to Cobbett, caused by "the fresh issues of paper money which accompanied the renewal of the Bank Protection Bill".[38] Harriet Martineau said that the "opinion which so generally obtained in 1816, [was] that the depreciation of the currency during the war, and the practical return to a real standard at the period of peace, was a main if not the sole cause of . . . distress and embarrassment . . .".[39]

Whatever the causes of the depression were at the end of the war, there is no doubt that farmers experienced great hardship and many of the smaller men went out of business. Once again *The Agricultural State of the Kingdom* is an invaluable source of information. At Melton, for instance, ten farms of from 300 to 600 acres in extent were unoccupied, and twenty-eight of from 150 to 300 acres were vacant in Ely. In 1812 and '13 there had been fifty-four arrests and seven executions for debt equalling £765 among farmers in the Isle, whereas in 1814 and '15 the figures had gone up to 203 arrests and sixty executions amounting to £18,522.[40]

The Isle of Ely was hit worse than any other area in East Anglia. Western conceded as much, and Harriet Martineau recorded the fact in words that seem to have been repeated by practically every popular nineteenth-century historian who mentioned the Ely and Littleport riots. It was "somewhat like Prospero's Isle", she wrote, where there "was everything advantageous to life, save means to live". Places in Huntingdon were almost as badly off. The following report is by no means exceptional.

The poor of Yelling, (containing about 4,000 inhabitants), in which Sir George Leeds has a large estate, is in a deplorable state : the clergymen and overseers of the parish attended the meeting of Magistrates, held on Saturday fortnight, at Huntingdon, to request them to decide who were to keep the poor from *starving,* as *all* the farmers *renting* land, except one, had thrown up their land, and left the parish![41]

It might be expected from all the above that at least some

dispossessed farmers were among the rioters of 1816. There are fairly complete lists of the people who were involved in the troubles at Ely and Littleport extant, and documents in the Assize Records and Treasury Solicitor's Papers at the Public Record Office enable one to identify most of the rioters elsewhere. None of them, however, with the exception of Henry Benson, who was a rather special case, and two other minor figures,[42] appear to have been (or were) farmers. This is not absolutely conclusive because a few people still remain names only, but it seems reasonable to infer that people of this kind would have come to the fore either because they would be natural leaders, or because they would have been held specially responsible by prosecuting counsel. Furthermore a close search of the advertisement columns in the local Press dealing with dispossessions, sales of agricultural implements and so on has failed to reveal any of the rioters among the unfortunate people being sold up. With the exception of one or two people who will be mentioned later, practically all those involved were agricultural labourers, or, at places like Norwich and Bury St. Edmunds, spinners or weavers made redundant by machinery.

CHAPTER FOUR

THE LIST OF the eighty or so prisoners fully committed for trial at the Special Assizes in Ely in May 1816 shows that almost all of them were landless agricultural labourers earning the wages described elsewhere. The local solicitor, in preparing his brief for the Crown, saw fit to comment on wages, parish relief and the ownership of cottages and gardens. Eleven were supposed to have had a cottage and garden of their own : Mark Benton, a mole-catcher, had "one rood of Hempland", and John Freeman had a house and eight acres of land; Richard Rutter possessed two cows, Philip Morris was alleged to have had "land and money out at interest" and four others had gardens. An explanation of much of the hostility of these people could well be found in the fact that, under the Poor Law, relief was denied to a person with property. To qualify for relief, men like Rutter would have had to sell their possessions.[1] No details like those on the Ely and Littleport rioters are available on people concerned in incidents elsewhere, but, on the whole, those involved at Downham Market, Brandon and Norwich were labourers, and what information is available on them will be given in full in the appendix.

The exceptions to the above are very interesting. Dr. Hobsbawm has called shoemakers the "typical working-class intellectuals" and R. J. White said that "wherever the spirit of reform is stirring we are likely to find a cobbler".[2] William Arnold, from Brandon, one of the chief culprits in the troubles there, was a shoemaker and among the eighty committed for the Ely and Littleport incidents, there were no fewer than six more—John Walton from Ely, William Beamiss senior, his son, William, Francis Torrington, John Morris and Thomas Gray from Littleport. Among other tradesmen involved were a potter from Ely, Thomas Hunt, a tailor from Littleport, whose income was insufficient to keep him off the parish, and Aaron Layton, "a master bricklayer" from Ely. Daniel Wilson from Littleport was a blacksmith whose trade would have been affected by the slump in the agricultural business, and William Sibley and William

Atkin, carpenters from Littleport and Ely respectively, were probably in the same plight. Edward Wilson, indicted for stealing beef and mutton at Downham, was another blacksmith, and William Tibbs and William Barrett, two characters tried for riots in Huntingdonshire, were respectively a bricklayer and a hodman.[3] William Gotobed was also a bricklayer and one, Morley, described to Sidmouth as a "violent character" responsible for stirring up trouble near Stonham, was a tailor from Finningham.[4] John Dennis of Littleport was a publican, someone who relied heavily upon the labourers for a living.

None of these people would have had difficulty in identifying themselves with the plight of the labourers, and as late as the 1870s tradesmen, shopkeepers and publicans could be found anxious and willing to lead labourers' movements in East Anglia. These were the people "above the rank of labourers" who were so often, and so wrongly, accused of being worse than the crowd and the sole instigators of the troubles. According to one early commentator "their motives must have been more than ordinarily malignant, their hearts depraved beyond the common standard of moral depravity, or their ignorance and liability to deception black beyond that of all their fellow creatures".

A number of the people described simply as labourers may well have been ex-servicemen recently returned to their villages. Demobilisation had been rapid and large numbers had been flocking back from the wars. Evidence from contemporary sources shows that they too were regarded as among the chief authors of the troubles of 1816. The Reverend James Buck said that, at Lavenham, "many military have returned to us of late, who have necessarily increased the great want of labour".[5] One of the earliest commentators on the Ely and Littleport riots seemed to suggest that discharged seamen and merchant seamen might have been present[6] and a narrative of the incidents drawn up by the Treasury Solicitor said quite definitely that the troublemakers were people just out of the militia who "disguised their intention under the mark of seeking a remedy from the distress they pretended to suffer from, the want of employment, the low price of labour and the high price of flour".[7] In the list of offenders to be tried at the Special Assizes only Joseph Stibbard, "Chelsea Pensioner", and Francis Torrington, the shoemaker, "Pension—Marine service", are definitely identifiable as persons with military experience, however. At Southerey ex-servicemen certainly were present, although their names are not definitely known, and "John Brown, a native of Ramsay, who has lately served as a private in the marines" was "one of the most forward" in the Huntingdonshire troubles.[8] Joseph Bugg was also an ex-serviceman,[9] and Henry Spendlove may well have been. All these will appear in the narrative later.

The ex-servicemen were certainly not the sole authors of the riots. But they were at least partly responsible for the form the riots took. No promises like those given to the servicemen of a century later were offered to veterans of the Napoleonic wars, but the reactions of the two groups were not unlike. Disillusionment on finding that unemployment and parish relief were the only rewards for war service must have turned scores into potential revolutionaries. At Littleport the rioters, as will be seen later, armed themselves in a most military-like fashion, and at Southerey a complete order of battle was drawn up. Philip Russell said that he heard

"William Hardy say that in case they [came] into action that day he had instructed the Party how to form themselves which was for the front Rank to be armed with Pitchforks and to place themselves upon one knee with the Fork Irons upwards to meet the cavalry the next Rank were to be armed with Long Duck guns to be supported upon the Shoulder of a Man and to be fired off by another man in the third Rank." Thirty to Forty guns were said to be available.[10]

Contemporary writers were under the impression that there was an organisation which spread over a large part of East Anglia and co-ordinated the trouble spots. A statement an Ely solicitor prepared for the prosecution said that "It has, indeed, been discovered that an intimate connection and secret communication existed between the two parishes [Littleport and Southerey], and that an organised system of riot and plunder, which was to have been carried into every parish in that quarter, had existed for some-days previously to the transactions we are about to relate".[11] On 27th May, a correspondent from Ely wrote to the Home Secretary saying that, for six or seven weeks, delegates from certain places had been going around stirring up trouble "and that a combination had taken place",[12] an opinion which was shared by the local Press and even repeated by Cobbett.[13] There is absolutely no evidence to substantiate these contentions, however, and they seem to have arisen out of a confusion over what happened in Littleport. There the rioters did set up an organisation, appoint a treasurer and perhaps even sent messengers to neighbouring villages, but these arrangements appear to have been made after the riots had begun. In fact, the one thing the whole rising in 1816 lacked was central, controlled leadership, something noted with relief by the authorities at the time.[14] The poor were being thrown together in the labour gangs where their grievances could have been aired with people from other parishes, but the comings and goings between villages beyond that were probably no more than those of usual times. Obviously the riots elsewhere were newsworthy and what happened a few miles away would excite the populace of other villages and put them into a more aggressive state of mind. One of the prosecutors at Ely recognised that the Littleport labourers were inspired by the apparently successful example of people elsewhere, but it is noticeable that neither he nor his colleagues produced any evidence of a very widespread organisation. The Duke of Grafton, Lord Lieutenant of Suffolk, had heard the stories but wrote to Sidmouth that "I am not disposed to think . . . that the disturbances or fires which have taken place are to be ascribed to any organised system . . ."[15]

Although there was no co-ordinated and widespread organisation, there were certainly secret meetings at a village level. In times of distress and unemployment, men are sure to congregate to air their grievances, and in the villages in the early nineteenth century there were ready-made organisations in which the labourers could meet.

It is difficult to avoid the inference that many of the trouble-makers in places like Brandon were members of poaching gangs. These abounded throughout the whole of the country and would consist of the more adventurous of the labourers.[16] As has been mentioned before, it seems to be no coincidence that an avowed aim of the rioters at Downham Market was to liberate a gang recently imprisoned. Penalties were becoming heavier and the poaching war more bitter. In many places practically the whole populace were poachers and their secret meetings were obvious places in which to talk of demonstrating against their lot. Grafton told Sidmouth[17] that, during the whole of the winter of 1815–16, secret meetings had been held throughout Suffolk and scores of anonymous placards were issued complaining of the labourers' lot. A Major Marrie also wrote a number of hysterical letters to the Home Secretary, many of which contain a great deal of information about his part of Suffolk. ". . . lights are seen in cottages all the night, which cannot be kept up without great expense if it is not paid for by secret agents", he wrote on 25th April.[18] Two days earlier he had said that he had heard that "Several parishes have been taking oaths to stand by each other as in the Mutiny at the Nore".[19] Bearing in mind how severe the legal penalties for seditious behaviour were in 1816, it is no cause for surprise that oaths were sworn. Marrie also sent a copy of an anonymous letter found in Bildeston church which supported his contention that whatever organisation there was included the neighbouring villages also. It read[20]

Gentlemen

I could wish to be very carefully about you buisness for indeed things are getting to a very bad pass for there is a great number of us thinking about making a bussel amongst you Gentlement.

an so. I Remain to

R x m (undecipherable)

are 3 parishes join

(our warning

729 men)

It is possible to discover some interesting information about the poaching gangs from local and national Press reports of the time. At the Gloucester Assizes in April, for instance, seven poachers were charged with having killed a gamekeeper. All were found guilty and sentenced to death, two suffering the extreme penalty. Charged with them was William Adams Broadribb, an attorney. He was alleged to have administered an illegal oath to the members of the gang swearing them "not to 'peach each other". The ceremony appears to have been a strange one, the prisoner saying "that the book upon which he swore the men was not a Testament, but an account book, entitled 'The Young Man's Best Companion' ". The swearing did Broadribb little good as one of the gang turned State's evidence and gave information which netted the attorney a sentence of seven years' transportation.[21]

There is more evidence of a poaching gang active in Essex early in 1816. On the 30th September of that year, a farmer of Elsenham was awakened and shot at by a gang which "had long been the terror of the neighbourhood, as poachers, sheep stealers, &c.". One of the organisations for prosecuting felons mentioned earlier, The Elsenham Association, then hired a Bow

Street runner. Within a couple of days he had apprehended two people, one of whom "*squeaked,* as is technically termed (became an evidence against the rest)" and this led to the arrest of the whole gang. They were brought before the Saffron Walden magistrates where it was said that the mother of some of the prisoners acted as "*artist,* when any robberies were committed; that she painted all their likenesses in *black,* to disguise their countenances, and gave them a tolerable portion of gin preparatory to their midnight adventures".[22]

The poachers were acquitted on a legal technicality and were eventually retried at the Chelmsford Assizes in March 1817. They were indicted for burglary at the house of John Dennis and three of the leaders were sentenced to death. The gang was said to consist of twelve regular members, including the mother and three of her sons. Of the three given the death penalty, Aaron Miller, William Griffin and Joseph Clark (two of whose sons were convicted of burglaries), only the latter was left for execution. He "was executed (at Chelmsford) on Friday se'nnight. He died very penitent : he made no confession, excepting what, from the enormity and nature of his offence, might be expected, that he had not attended a place of worship, from the age of 14, to the time of his death".[23] ". . . six witnesses were . . . called, who all swore that (William) Griffin and Miller, on the night of the robbery, and at the time the accomplice[24] swore they were at Mrs. Clark's, were at their club, at the *Boar's Head,* Bishops Stortford."[25]

The clubs of the kind that Griffin and Miller were supposed to have been at were even more likely than the poaching gangs to have been the centres of sedition at a village level. This was realised by contemporaries. Friendly Societies, or Box or Benefit Clubs, as they were more generally called, were very common throughout the whole country, and it did not escape notice that the rioters at Littleport issued forth on their quest for violence from *The Globe* public house, where they had been attending a meeting of their club.

These clubs, of which Sir Frederick Eden was a great supporter,[26] were suspect to the authorities for many years before 1816. In Essex they were particularly well established, and the Rev. G. Howlett wrote of one in his own parish of Dunmow. It accepted members between the ages of eighteen and thirty-five and had been in existence for thirty years when he wrote. It had eighty members in 1801 and during its life fifty-seven people had been expelled. £706 1s. 8d. had been paid out to sick members and the Club still had £137 11s. 8d. in hand. £120 of that was used to purchase £200 worth of stock in 3 per cent consols which raised the last figure, with interest, to about £143. Howlett went on to point out that no less than £312 12s. 3d. had been spent on drink.[27] The Dunmow Club may have been an exceptionally wealthy one, but, apart from that, it was typical of its kind.

The rules and orders of the very club that the Littleport rioters attended are still in existence,[28] and they show that it, too, conformed to the general pattern. Started in 1785, it was restricted to Littleport people. There was a five-shilling entrance fee and members paid 8d. per meeting. Beneficiaries out of work or incapacitated received 7s. a week.[29]

The Articles of the original Friendly Society of Cambridge are also extant. Its membership was restricted to persons aged between twenty and thirty and anyone not capable of earning 18s. a week "or had ill health", or who was a landlord of a public house, a brewer's servant, bailiff or "bailiff's follower", soldier, sailor, gentleman's servant or member of another club was forbidden entry. If a member entered the militia or the regular service he was to be excluded! Subscriptions were 1s. 6d. a month for the club plus 6d. for beer "and every absent member's beer money shall be spent; every member present shall receive a medal for his beer and pay one penny; and any member that spends his money out of the Club-room shall forfeit threepence". The scales of relief were given in detail.[30]

Every club, except those specifically for women, met in a public house, and it was because they led to drunkenness that they were criticised so frequently. Howlett, after saying that they gave relief as a *"right"*, in contrast to the poor law which gave only *"discretionary* provision attended with an abundance of distressing and mortifying treatment",[31] went on to point out that, whenever the clubs met, there was a beer allowance and that heavy drinking inevitably ensued. "But besides regular periodical meetings," he added, "they have likewise their grand anniversary festivals, at which all the members are assembled from every quarter; and this, it has often been remarked, sometimes occasions two or three days of idleness, dissipation, and drunkenness." "Notwithstanding their superficial flattering appearance, they may have been highly pernicious; they may have contributed to

the increase of idleness and intemperance; prevented the diminution of ale houses, given occasion to illegal combinations, and
seditious proceedings; caused much more misery and wretchedness than they have ever relieved . . ."[32]

It is not likely that the agricultural labourer gained much
financial benefit from membership of a Box Club, but it did provide him with a meeting place at which freemason-like secrecy
was observed, and at which his grievances could be aired without fear of the wrath of his employer descending upon him. Of
course, it is impossible to prove that the clubs were the centres
of village disaffection, but that they were is more than just possible. Arthur Young, in another oft-quoted remark, revealed
much about the labourer's attitude to life and why he chose beer-
house society so frequently:

"Go to an ale-house kitchen of an old enclosed county," he said,
"and there you will see the origin of poverty and the poor-rates. For
whom are they to be sober? For whom are they to save? (such are
their questions). For the parish? If I am diligent, shall I have leave
to build a cottage? If I am sober, shall I have land for a cow? If I
am frugal, shall I have half an acre of potatoes? You offer no
motives; you have nothing but a parish officer and a workhouse.
Bring me another pot."[33]

It is perhaps a cause of some surprise to find that the authorities did not resort to using *agents-provocateurs* in the rural areas.
It is well known that the Government of the day were not beyond
doing this and it has already been mentioned that the gentlemen
of Downham Market successfully infiltrated an agent into a
poaching gang. The riots did not break with such suddenness
that there was not time to plant people, but the fact remains
that none were used. Lord Sidmouth was urged by the
indefatigable Major Marrie to do so nevertheless. ". . . some
clever persons disguised as labourers," he wrote, "might be the
means of discovering the incendiaries."[34]

Nonconformist meetings were regarded by those in power with
some of the suspicion that Benefit Clubs and public house meetings were, and accusations that dissenters were behind the
troubles were heard when the time came to apportion the blame
for the riots of 1816. The labourers *en masse* then were as hostile
to the Church of England as they were forty years later, when
the author of the religious census described them as "unconscious
secularists" whose "dislike for the particular vessels of Christian-

ity seldom became a generalised fundamentalist rejection of religion itself".[35] When they went to worship they preferred to go to chapel, but their opportunities were few in 1816. Wesley had had little effect in East Anglia, as the Minutes of the Methodist Conference show. The Wesleyans had few buildings and small congregations, and none of the preachers named as stationed in the area took part in the riots (or their suppression).[36] In Norwich, where the accusations against the nonconformists were bad enough for a public denial in the Press,[37] the Wesleyans numbered 700 in 1819. In Ely, despite Edmund Carter's claim that "no other City but Ely . . . can boast, as they truly can, that it hath no other congregation but that of the Established Church", there were 452 Methodists according to the returns for 1815.[38]

The Wesleyans, or members of any of the old dissenting congregations, were unlikely to have supported the rioters, even although they were regarded with suspicion by the authorities. The years 1815–16, however, were years of tremendous activity among the Primitives, or Ranters, a radical group which had broken away frrom the parent body and which was attracting great attention in the Midlands. They were the people most likely among the religious to have supported the rioters, and may have been the people alleged to have been among the trouble-makers in 1816. Unfortunately there are no adequate studies of Primitive Methodism in the locality, or for that matter on a national scale, and so it is impossible to do much more than note the fact that the movement became strong in the area a few years later. There is every possibility that the people who were to form the congregations then had already broken with the Wesleyans and were meeting in private, where they could indeed have discussed insurrection. One piece of evidence from the Press, however, suggests that the Primitives were active in the area earlier than their historians have suggested.[39] In July Robert Newstead, a Methodist preacher, was prosecuted by the Reverend Algernon Peyton, of Doddington, for preaching to a crowd of people "otherwise than according to the liturgy and practice of the Church of England, in a field which had not been licensed", and in a way popular among Primitives. The magistrates very sensibly dismissed the charge.[40]

Only one of the correspondents, Beckett, a magistrate, wrote to the Home Secretary during the troubles of 1816 mentioning a dissenter who was prominent on the side of the labourers. James Smythe, "a petty attorney at Brandon, clerk to the Justice's

Bench", was said to have had "Justice by the nose. Mr. Smythe is moreover a little dissenting preacher", the letter went on. "He mixes constantly with all the poor and profligate characters of Brandon, and unless he be grievously belied is deeply connected with them . . . There are many grounds for suspicion against this Mr. Smythe."[41] What these grounds of suspicion were are unknown, as Smythe appears to have behaved quite properly during the incidents in Brandon.[42]

None of this is enough to assign the dissenters a part in the story of the riots of the summer of 1816. It is certain that the authorities would have made an example of any of them taken into custody, and during none of the trials were any charges made against the religious. Instead the labourer's hostility to the Church and clergy and his *lack* of religion was emphasised.

CHAPTER FIVE

THE CHURCH OF ENGLAND held no attraction for the labourers in the early nineteenth century. It was an organisation that was incredibly wealthy, and was peopled by vicars who, as often as not, did not live with their flocks. Henry Bate Dudley, whose part in suppressing the Ely riots will be described later, and who was "collated to a prebendal stall in the Cathedral Church of Ely" in May 1815 lost £28,000 in trying to obtain a living in Essex,[1] and was one of the people who contributed to the popular impression of his Church. Poor clergymen there undoubtedly were, but as in the case of enclosures, it was the general impression they gave that influenced people's attitudes. Gunning described "Billy" Moore, a Suffolk clergyman, "a great favourite with the country gentlemen, by whom his society was much sought; for he kept an excellent hunter, rode well up to the hounds, drank very hard". "He sang an excellent song, danced remarkably well, so that the young ladies considered no party complete without him." He had entered the Church solely to extricate himself from financial difficulties and conformed to the popular opinion of a rural clergyman.[2] The local Press often carried reports of the wrongdoings of clergy and the following extract of what happened at a country service warrants inclusion. In the very issue that contained the first reports of the riot at Brandon *The Cambridge Gazette* said that the[3]

Parish-clerk of a neighbouring village on Sunday last, after offering too liberally at the shrine of Bacchus, during the church service fell into the arms of Morpheus, to the great disappointment of his Reverence the Rector, who, after waiting with great patience for some time for the responses, gently tapped Master Moses on the shoulder, when, after a few gasps and shrugs, "Richard was himself again", and the service went regularly on.

No records of church attendances were gathered for another half-century, but it is clear that the East Anglian labourers rarely went, particularly when "living in" began to decline. Reporters to the Board of Agriculture often commented on their non-attendance, and some idea of just how poorly attended churches were might be gauged from the comment of a reporter on *The Cambridge Gazette* who said that in the countryside they "were worse attended on the day of Thanksgiving [for the end of the war] than were ever known on any occasion".[4] Mr. Vachell, the Vicar of Littleport, who was an object of obvious hatred to the labourers, had small congregations. Long after the riots were over, it was reported that "The Rev. Mr. Thickens who has had the care of the parish of Littleport since the riots of May last" would leave after the 23rd April 1817. "The Sunday evening congregation, which used to be about 30 or 40, besides a few rude and uneducated children, is now, we are told, seldom less than three or four hundred."[5] The last figures would seem to err on the optimistic side.

Clergymen were among the chief objects of the rioters' attention in May for at every turn they appeared as opponents of the poor. Not only did they have what was considered a sinecure, but they completely identified themselves with the interests of the ruling classes in the villages. As often as not they were among the guardians and overseers of the poor and usually had control over the village charities: Matthew Bateman's charity at Upwell, for instance, set up to provide clothes for the poor, was administered by the Rev. E. Pemberton; one of those at Lawshall was administered by the Minister and churchwardens only; at Hadleigh there were thirty-two charities in 1816, all controlled by the Rector, the Rectors of Semer and Elmet, another Reverend gentleman and six others, while at Kettlebaston two were administered by "The Minister, churchwardens and overseers"; at Brandon it was the same story, and at Clare all the charities were run by either the Vicar, or the churchwardens, "and Principal Inhabitants".[6] The maladministration of village charities is vitally important in explaining the rise of village unionism in the 1870s and there is little doubt that they were run, if not dishonestly, then quite as selfishly in 1816.

Clergymen were also in a majority on the bench of magistrates. People whose main concern was the cure of souls were called upon to administer a harsh and unyielding law that could have no other effect but make them hated. Rural crime of all kinds was on the increase[7] and many of the clergymen were zealous in their determination to put it down by imposing heavy sentences. The Rev. J. Vachell was an unpopular magistrate of this kind and Henry Bate Dudley was another. *The Examiner* carried an article on "Magisterial severity" which is only extraordinary for the fact that it involved a prominent person who could be held up to ridicule. A "Reverend Magistrate" in Middlesex sentenced "Anne Green and her Daughter . . . to *One Year's Imprisonment, for breaking off the limb of a walnut-tree with intent to take it away, and for having actually carried off some branches of the said tree"*. The tree belonged to C. Dundas, the M.P. for Berkshire, who, *The Examiner* said, "acquiesced in the late proposal for adding to the income of the Duke of Cumberland. His Royal Honour, in Mr. Dundas's opinion, was fully justified in attempting to get some extra thousands from the people to assist in boiling the Royal kettle; but Anne Green, in wishing to heat hers at the Hon. Member's cost, deserves a year's imprisonment. Is not this zeal for rank, and this indignation against pauper delinquency somewhat immoderate?" the journal asked.[8] Dundas demanded a public apology. This was refused, but "If the Hon. Member" would procure "the discharge of Widow Green and her daughter with a babe at her breast", the article went on, "the Publisher of *The Examiner* will forward to him his best *thanks,* if he will deign to accept them".[9]

The clergy received their fair share of threats and threatening letters. Thomas Hunt, after helping break into the Vicar's house at Littleport, summed up his attitude when he said, "Damn all the Parsons to Hell, they don't subscribe anything towards the maintenance of the poor", and a threatening letter found in Lawshall said that three houses there were to be set alight "and the parson to be burnt in his bed".[10] James Tobias Cook, a clergyman magistrate from Whittlesea, sent Sidmouth a copy of one he had received. The unprintable parts establish that some present-day obscenities are at least 150 years old. "Mr. Cook," it said,

this is to let you no that you are a dam bad un but we will fit you for it we will save [serve] you as we did oer Mr. Vachel of Littleport and ten times worse for you may expect it next for you are a dam bad un but you will rue for it and then you will be sorey for what you have don for you shall have your house puld down and all Wittlesee burning down and that you shall see before long if we live for you are all a damnd bad and you may find me out if you can . . . but you cannot for you are a fool and a dam bad un.[11]

The labourers in the Isle of Ely had a special reason for hating the Church. It was the owner of vast amounts of land, and not

only did the magistrates' bench consist mainly of pluralist clergy
but they, and other officials, were also appointed directly by the
Bishop—not above suspicion for chicanery himself[12]—who
exercised secular jurisdiction in the area until 1836.[13] The Isle
had its own Assizes and Chief Justice, and the Church was seen
in the rôle of an all-pervading oppressor of the poor. What
justice there was was clergyman's justice.

There were attempts by the labourers in a few places to enlist
farmers to their side by attacking the clergy and promising to
have the tithe abolished. This failed for a number of reasons.
First of all it was not an unbearable burden in England,[14]
and quite a number of the clergy voluntarily relinquished their
claims during the period of distress—Townley of Upwell for
instance.[15] In any case the farmers were among the most enthusi-
astic members of the Church and many of them were tenants of
the Church. Nevertheless, according to Major Marrie, "the
mob" said to the farmers in his area that "if you will join us we
will lower the tithe, and then corn will be cheaper, and we shall
get work".[16] Near Wattisham[17] a farmer, again according to
Marrie, seemed disposed to sanction a riot and said that he
blamed the clergy and tithes for his predicament[18] but he took
no part in the movement. In fact, one looks in vain for either a
farmer or clergyman who appeared as even moderately disposed
towards the labourers until the troubles were all over. The Rev.
Dr. Robert Chatfield of Chatteris sent "an address to the Inhabitants of the Isle of Ely" to the magistrates in May 1816 which
contained all the sanctimonious preaching which the labourers
regarded as typical mockery. Chatfield asked for it to be printed
and distributed (it was not); it concluded

. . . let us study the lessons of that Book, which has been so diffused
amongst all classes, that even the most ignorant cannot plead their
want of knowledge. The Bible, that best hope and anchor of the
poor, that sweetest source of consolation in adversity, commands
you to be wise and peaceful and temperate,—to walk humbly in
your several callings to practice then the truths which it inculcates,
and you will find a place in your hearts above all prizes, a confidence
in the Most High—support in every trial in this world, and the
bright assurance of another and a better

A friend of the Poor.[19]

Chatfield's appeal would have had little effect, even if it had
been published. An enormous number of the labourers were illit-

erate with little or no interest in any kind of religion. The populace of the fens, according to Lord Suffield, was composed "of persons wholly uninformed, uncultivated and rude in their manners and of turbulent and riotous dispositions"[20] who, as Arthur Young said, rarely saw the inside of a church. The rioters who were hanged at Ely signed a confession in which they acknowledged some religious beliefs, but it does not have the ring of truth about it. Daniel Harwood and Thomas Thody, who were executed for their part in the Downham riots, were more truthful. "We are authorised to state," announced a Norfolk newspaper, "that none of these unfortunate men had ever made any profession of religion among any body of Christians; but, on the contrary, they acknowledged that they had lived in an awful neglect of religious duties, and had been sinking in sin prior to their commission of those crimes which brought them to their untimely end."[21] Joseph Clark, the Elsenham poacher, made a similar confession that is quoted elsewhere.

A nearly illiterate peasantry then looked upon the landowners, churchmen and farmers (and of course the millers) as one group, and it was easy for them to go on from there to regard the distress they suffered from as being deliberately brought about. Their poor relief was kept as low as possible, the clergy told them to put up with their lot, they were forbidden to take the game they considered was common property, they had witnessed selfish campaigns to alter the corn laws and abolish taxes and then prices began to rise. By May 1816 the cost of a quartern loaf (4 lbs. 5½ oz.) fixed at the Assize of Bread in Cambridge was 11¾d., and the price of a quartern of wheat had risen by 18s. in three weeks.[22] Against these increases the labourers finally rebelled. Violence seemed to be the only way to combat a harsh and entrenched tyranny. They were familiar with force and now was the desperate time to use it in their own interests. "The people who endured the reign of Castlereagh came of a stock which knew familiarly the menace of the pressgang, the gallows and the lash. They had lived in a world where man-made violence ranked with the fell forces of nature."[23] William Dawson, a rioter at Downham who was not prosecuted, was heard to say "that he had been working for a long time for a small allowance, and as he was between Earth and Sky he would either have some remedy or lose his life".[24] Richard Rutter summed up the whole desperate plight and the state of mind of the labourers when he told the Rev. Law, a magistrate, that "It was nothing to him (that many of the Littleport people had gone home) he was starved and he would be damned if he would not be fed".[25]

It is noticeable that, although the labourers, among whom was a leavening of skilled artisans, took up arms in 1816, they had no avowed political motives, except in the special sense mentioned earlier. So complete was the tyranny of the countryside that they seemed to think that they could wring concessions from the magistrates, and, even more pathetically, that these would be kept. At a time when freehold estates were advertised for sale under the heading *Votes for the County of Huntingdon* the labourers showed no realisation of the need for parliamentary reform, although occasionally they held forth about place-men. Thomas Hunt, the Littleport tailor, talking to Thomas Waddelow, showed how he equated the Church and the Government, and then gave voice to the only intimation that the labourers ever thought they might have to do more than fight the magistrates and farmers: "We have got thro' the business very well," he said. On being told that the concessions the rioters had gained at Ely might not be kept, he told Waddelow that in that case "you must join us and make those damned Parsons and these great men come down, and we must go up above and pull that great House down". "Meaning," the statement went on, "as this Deponent understood the Parliament House."[26]

Only in Norwich of all the affected places was there a populace which showed political inclinations. This is explained by the presence of a depressed manufacturing population which had an extraordinarily rich and long history of radical, trade union, and Jacobin tradition, and was, moreover, prone to riot at the slightest provocation. In the late 1830s a witness described the turbulent city as "From top to bottom . . . dominated by party considerations", with "incessant elections" which produced a "demoralising pandemonium of bribery and treating, intimidation and personal violence". In these conditions the woollen workers, once able to bargain with the masters, fought violently against the introduction of machinery and wage cutting. "Vitriolthrowing, window breaking, and violent picketing were of common occurrence" whenever feelings ran high.[27] In March 1815, for instance, the Brunswick Hussars had to disperse a mob which had attacked Lord Albemarle and T. W. Coke, M.P., because they had supported the Corn Bill.[28] During the 1816 riots, however, no political slogans were apparent, even although a movement to stage a demonstration was then afoot in the city, as the following republican placard shows.[29] What was being proposed was that the people of Norwich should follow the example of numerous other groups who were marching to the capital. (A group of Bilston colliers, for instance, were dragging carts laden with coal behind them and attracting a considerable amount of publicity to themselves.)[30]

Attention

Fellow countrymen & Slaves, now is the time to shake of your Load of Oppression & Starvation for which Purpose meet on the Castle Hill on Sunday Morning at 10 o'clock then March to London there Demand your Rights like Sons of Liberty.

God Save the People ! !

Enough has been said about the background to the riots and the conditions under which the labourers involved lived and grew up. Before describing the actual course they took, it might be as well to sum up all that has gone before in the labourers' own words. The anonymous letter addressed "To the Gentlemen of Ashill" went as follows (a few words are undecipherable).[31]

This is to inform you that you have by this time brought us under the heaviest burden and under the hardest yoke we ever knowed; it is too hard for us to bear; you have often times blinded us saying that the fault was all in the Place-men of Parliament : but now you have opened our eyes, we know they have a great power, but they have nothing to do with the regulation of this parish.

You do as you like, you rob the poor of their commons right, plough the grass up that God send to grow, that a poor man may feed a cow, Pig, Horse, nor Ass; lay muck and stones on the road to prevent the grass growing. If a poor man is out of work and wants a day or two's work you will give him 6d. per week, and then a little man that does not employ a labourer at all, must help pay for your work doing, which will bring them chargeable to the parish. There is 5 or 6 of you have gotten all the whole of the land in this parish in your own hands and you would wish to be rich and starve all the other part of the poor of the parish. If any poor man wanted anything, then you will call a Town meeting about it, to hear which could continue to hiss him the most, which have caused us to have a county meeting, to see if we cannot gain some redress.

Gentlemen, these few lines are to inform you that God Almighty have brought our blood to a proper circulation, that have been in a very bad state a long time, and now without an alteration of the foresaid, we mean to circulate your blood with the leave of God. And we do not intend to give you but a very short time to consider about it, as we have gotten one or two of the head, on our side. There was 2 cows and an Ass feeding on the road last Saturday, and there was 2 farmers went to the keepers and said they would pound them, if they did not drive them away, one of them candidly (?) went home, got a plough and horses, and ploughed the grass up that growed on the road.

We deem the miller to be full as big a rogue as you farmers for the wheat raise 1s. per Comb. He will then raise 2d. per stone; so we shall drive the whole   before us and knock down the Mill, and set fire to all   houses and stacks as we go along : we shall begin in the Night.

And the first Man that refuses to join the Combination shall suffer death in a moment, or the first person that is catched saying anything against the same, shall suffer death. We have had private ambushes around us for some time, and by this time you will find it is coming to a point.

Take notice that this is a private letter wrote at this time, but we fear it will be too public for your profits : so we wish to prepare yourselves ready for action; for we intend to have things as we like; you have had a good long time. We have counted up that we have gotten about 60 of us to 1 of you : therefore should you govern, so many to one? No : we will fight for it and if you win the day, so be it.

Swines, Fokelee, Moocher————.

PART TWO

CHAPTER SIX

THE FARMERS' AGITATIONS in East Anglia which, it has been maintained, influenced the labourers, have already been dealt with. These increased in severity from 1814 onwards and were very shortly followed by more specifically working-class disturbances. In December of that year, for instance, sailors rioted for higher wages in King's Lynn and had to be dispersed by the Brunswick Hussars,[1] and four months later three people were charged with having taken part in another riot in which they attempted to demolish the gaol in the same town.[2] The troubles involving Coke in Norwich have been mentioned. One of James Buxton's labourers, in Essex, when told of the fact that his wages were to be cut, replied that there was "a blaze" in Norwich and that the labourers might soon follow the example set in that city.[3]

One of the earliest riots in the train of events that culminated in the serious risings of May 1816 took place in Suffolk, in the parish of Gosbeck. There a crowd of about twenty men gathered together on a Saturday in March 1815 and proceeded to smash farm machinery. Eight of them were taken to Ipswich gaol and confronted with the magistrates. A crowd assembled outside and when one of the J.P.s tried to leave he was pelted and had to take refuge in *The Great White Horse Inn*. There he had to stay until ten o'clock at night when he was escorted away by constables and dragoons.[4]

In the summer of 1815 similar troubles occurred in Suffolk again. In August Daniel Grimwood and eleven others[5] were charged at the Ipswich Quarter Sessions with rioting and smashing machinery, the property of John Roper, in the parish of Holbrook. For this, all were found guilty and received sentences ranging from four to twelve months. Usually the labourers had little to say in their own defence but the following report sums up their attitude:

Mr. Storks, for the prosecution, insisted upon the urgent necessity of supporting the laws, and after the evidence, which was full and conclusive, had been gone through, the prisoners were called

upon for their defence, but they had little to urge except the
difficulty of gaining employment, which they attributed to the use
of machines . . .[6]

In the same edition of the newspaper containing the above
was the report of another trial at the Woodbridge Quarter Sessions in which Edmund Prime and six others[7] were tried for
machine breaking in the parishes of Kenton and Mon-soham. All
were found guilty; six were given a year's imprisonment and one
six months. The report concluded : "It is much to be hoped that
these necessary examples will have the effect of preventing such
excesses for the future—excesses not only disastrous to the objects
of them, but ruinous to the perpetrators." They certainly did not
do that.

The implements in these cases were threshing machines. As
should have been made clear from the description of the background to the troubles of 1816, the farmers had plenty of purely
economic and selfish motives for sacking labourers, but, added to
these, was the availability in these years of new machines capable
of saving enormous expense in labour costs. The labourers' reactions were exactly the same as those of the Luddites and the
hand loom weavers. Frederick Coventry, a young officer sent to
enquire about the cause of some trouble at Clare, reported to his
commanding officer that the poor "hate[d]" the threshing machines "beyond all things".[8]

There is no doubt that the introduction of the mills, as they
were usually called, from the end of the eighteenth century did
make work more difficult to find and aggravated conditions from
1814 onwards. Over much of East Anglia threshing by the flail
had been practically the only winter employment (the Gosbeck
incident took place during the winter season), but the reports of
the Board of Agriculture show that this work was increasingly
being done mechanically. In his review of Norfolk in 1804
Arthur Young dealt at considerable length with the way machines were being introduced there. Coke of Holkham had one, for
instance; Colonel Buller of Haydon had one operated by steam;
and a Mr. Johnson of Kempston had one requiring six to eight
horses, six men and one woman to work it, which threshed more
cheaply and cleanly than flails.[9] In Essex the situation was the
same : John Vaizey, an object of considerable animosity, had
erected a mill at Halstead and Dr. Asplin at Little Wakering
had a machine worked by a man and two boys and a little girl

who drove the horse. In the early years of their history the machines, which were extremely expensive, had been unreliable, but the initial mechanical troubles were being solved by about 1807. Spurgeon of Bradwell told Young that "last year's wheat which was badly done [by hand] at 2s. a quarter, was done by the machine perfectly well". A correspondent of a Colchester newspaper, who advocated the abandonment of threshing machines, said that one of four to five horse power would thresh as much corn in one day as twenty men working with the flail.[10]

With the exception of a few possible cases of arson, for instance in St. Ives (where a barn was burnt down "presumably through malice to Mrs. Giffard, the owner of the barn"),[11] at Helmingham (Norfolk)[12] and in the Hundred of Plomesgate (Suffolk), there were no more cases of agrarian rioting reported in East Anglia until April 1816. In that month the prices of flour and bread began to rise, and this was the immediate cause of the demonstrations. In this they were exactly like the better-known and well-publicised riots at Bridport.[13] At first they were of a secret, purely negative kind, but eventually the news that labourers were stirring themselves spread over the whole of Eastern England and they became more cohesive, more violent, better supported and ended in the serious conflicts at Norwich, Downham Market, Brandon and Ely.

In Essex the first outbreak seems to have occurred on Sunday, 14th April, at Mile End Heath, near Colchester, when James Posford's threshing tackle was smashed and fired,[14] but no culprits were brought to book. Later in the month a malt kiln was fired at Maunden, near Bishop's Stortford, and the blaze spread to the nearby Maunden Hall, doing £15,000 worth of damage. For this offence Joseph Bugg (or Bagg) was hunted and arrested by Charles Moor, an agent of the insurers, the Suffolk Fire Office, and eventually appeared at the County Assizes. Bugg, who was twenty-six years of age and an ex-serviceman who had fought in Spain, claimed that he was drunk when he committed the offence and that James Glandfield, the owner of the kiln, was the worst possible kind of farmer. The Judge, however, held forth on the "depravity and wickedness" of incendiaries, the "heinousness" of Bugg's crimes and the need to make an example of him. He was hanged at Ipswich on 24th August.[15]

There were no incidents reported from Cambridgeshire during April, but in Huntingdon a field of standing reeds, the property of General Hussey, was burnt in Wood Walton Fen.[16]

In Suffolk, premises at Bungay were fired at 2 a.m. on Friday, the 26th. The *Bury and Norwich Post,* which carried good reports of these early incidents, was at pains to point out the futility of the labourers' actions as most of the property they were destroying was insured by the Suffolk Fire Office. On the 22nd May it also reminded its readers of the provisions of 9th Geo. 1, cap. 22 ("commonly called the black act") whereby the Hundred in which a fire was started by an incendiary was liable to make good the loss if it did not exceed £200. (If, however, the offender was caught and gaoled within six months the Hundred was not liable!) This part of the *Post*'s advice did not go unheeded. The Rev. Vachell took action under the law, and so did Henry Luffe, who sued the Hundred of Plomesgate in April 1817 and was awarded £200 for a barn burnt in November 1815.[17]

Most of the incidents in April occurred in Suffolk, and practically all of them were in the vicinity of Bury St. Edmunds. At Great Barton a cottage was maliciously burnt down for no apparent reason, and in Timworth a haulm stack was destroyed. At Grundisburgh and Groton more cottages were demolished, and at Hadleigh farm buildings were set alight. These all happened late in the month and were obviously inspired by what had been happening in a group of villages just to the south of Bury.

Gedding was the first of the group to see trouble. On the 17th April an enormous crowd assembled there and proceeded to smash threshing machines and mole ploughs, the property of Samuel Hustler. For these offences almost fifty people were brought before the Bury magistrates at the Quarter Sessions in July. The Reverend George Stone, the chairman, who seems to have thought, like Burke, that British government was nigh perfect, took the opportunity during his address to the Grand Jury to launch a typical attack on the labourers. In words quite remote from reality, he said they were trying to gain by violence

that relief of wants and redress of grievances which they ought to have sought by peaceable, orderly and legal application . . . The process of obtaining relief or redress by application, first to a parish officer, and afterwards to a magistrate is so plain, so easy, and so generally understood, that there can be no plea for resorting to any other means.[18]

The Norfolk Chronicle (25th May) chided the labourers in the

same way at the height of the troubles in May. While they
"admit[ted]" that "at this time they suffer from want of
employ", they should, the article went on, "trust in Providence
and look forward with hope to better days and . . . submit to
temporary deprivation".

The mole ploughs destroyed at Gedding were regarded by the
labourers with as much hatred as the threshing mills, and with
good reason. The implement was used during drainage operations, particularly on the heavy lands in Essex and Suffolk where
the troubles of April and May started. Young's survey of Essex
gives an idea of how the plough was being perfected during the
first decade of the nineteenth century and displacing agricultural labourers. Newman of Hornchurch had an early one of
inferior design with no wheels which had to be pulled by no less
than fourteen oxen. Later John Vaizey of Halstead, already
unpopular because of his use of threshing machines, was responsible for innovations which increased efficiency, and so too was
a Mr. Knight of Thaxted. He reported that his machine did the
job of draining ten acres of land at "$\frac{3}{4}$ of a rod asunder, or
twelve acres at one entire rod" for £3 17s. od. whereas "the
same quantity done in the usual way with the spade" cost £30,
"so that there is a saving of expense of more than 700 per
cent".[19] Although the ploughs still needed quite a large number
of labourers to tend them they did the work hitherto done by
hand (and on piece rates!) more quickly. Rightly or wrongly, the
labourers thought the ploughs were a cause of unemployment,
and in this the Rev. Mr. Buck of Lavenham agreed with them.[20]

Within a few days of the riot at Gedding, trouble spread to the
neighbouring villages. This was the area in which the frightened
Major Marrie lived and where he said midnight oaths were being
sworn. The close proximity of the trouble spots to each other
and the obvious fact that all the labourers knew each other and
what was going on, was probably the reason for the claims
already mentioned (and dismissed) that the incidents were cen-
trally directed. No reliable evidence to suggest that there was
more than the crudest getting together and that they were anything other than spontaneous hunger riots perpetrated by people
who saw their neighbours doing the same thing has come to
hand. "When a number of persons are assembled together with
such a spirit," the Rev. G. Stone told the Grand Jury at Bury,
"the example and intemperate language of some excites and
encourages others; the passions of the whole are enflamed, and

who is to say to what extremities and outrage they will not proceed."[21] The authorities prosecuted a group of labourers for an incident at Wattisham where they were alleged to have taken part in the formation of a village "trades union", but could not get evidence enough to convict more than one man. The magistrates of Cosford Hundred also met on the 27th April and said that they could find evidence of neither combinations nor the nocturnal meetings that so bothered the Major.[22]

Wattisham, a little village of about 170 inhabitants about five miles from Gedding, was the scene of great activity on the 23rd and 24th of April. Bills demanding vengeance or higher wages were posted up, and it was here that the offer was made to combine with farmers against the clergy, with but one lukewarm response.[23] The people of Wattisham visited the nearby village of Hitcham and violence ensued. Marrie, who had not been to bed for four nights and who had posted a night watch on his property at Bildeston (which he "fully believe[d] . . . of little avail, as from *compositions* (which now appears, all the country people are aware of) they can do any damage they please by laying the train at any opportunity . . .")[24] wrote to Sidmouth that, as he was composing his letter, "I am . . . in view of a farmhouse where the stacks, Barns and buildings have been set on fire". One hundred acres of corn were also ablaze.[25]

For the Wattisham incidents William Edwards, William Abbott and John Payne were charged at the Bury Quarter Sessions in August "For conspiring with several others, with a view of inducing labourers to form themselves into a society for raising their wages, &c., at Wattisham and elsewhere".[26] No evidence of this organisation, if it existed, has come to hand. No true bills were found against Abbott and Payne, but Edwards was given a sentence which should have successfully stopped him as an agitator for a couple of years afterwards. Fined one shilling, he also got nine months' imprisonment and was ordered to find sureties afterwards, himself in £30 and two others of £10 each to keep the peace for twelve months. Perhaps, to add point to the contention that there were no agitators or "delegates" going the rounds, it might be mentioned here that most of the people eventually prosecuted were not apprehended for some days after the incidents in which they took part. They would, in fact, have had time to go elsewhere and organise other demonstrations, yet a study of the charge sheets at the sessions and assizes shows only one person (Thomas Sindall) involved at more than one place (that is except at Ely and Littleport, which, as will be seen later, were inseparable).

While the troubles at Wattisham were taking place there was a similar incident a few miles away at Rattlesden. There Robert Leader ("styled commander") and a large crowd assembled and destroyed a mole plough, the property of Benjamin Morgan, a farmer of Gedding. Morgan must have been a very brave man for the troubles at Rattlesden were more violent than any so far. He was later complimented by the chairman of the Bench of Magistrates for his courage in resisting the crowd, and Marrie said that he "risqued his life alone" when facing a mob of 200 and more. It appears from the Quarter Sessions records that the crowd also attempted to rescue some of their number who had been imprisoned, but this charge was not pressed and so there are no details. Leader was fined one shilling and gaoled for two years; six were given a similar fine with a year's imprisonment; one was acquitted; four were discharged on their own recognizances of £10 to keep the peace; and nineteen were ordered to find sureties to keep the peace especially against Benjamin Morgan or serve three months.[27]

After the troubles at Wattisham, Rattlesden and Gedding, riots took place everywhere in the area. At Kettlebaston, on the 26th, a stack was fired for which Thomas Baker was committed, and at Welnetham threshing tackle belonging to John or Samuel Fenton was destroyed, for which four labourers eventually received prison sentences.[28] On Saturday, 27th, more tackle was destroyed at Cockfield.[29] These incidents caused considerable alarm in the county and the magistrates, mainly clergymen who, according to Marrie, were too terrified to act when action would have prevented the trouble spreading,[30] met in general session at Bury on Monday, 29th. As a result of this meeting a proclamation (see page 76) appeared in the public notices column of the local Press.[31]

This magistrates' proclamation had little effect and incidents occurred over much of West Suffolk and neighbouring parts of Essex during the first two weeks of May. In Ilminster Long Chandler's premises were burnt, and at Drinkstone, near the trouble centres of Rattlesden and Gedding, Joshua Grigby's barn was "wilfully set on fire" on the 3rd, and a £200 reward offered to anyone who caught the offenders. On the same night, John Pryke's stacks at Wickhambrook lit the sky, and outhouses of a farm occupied by Thomas Nottige at Henham

SUFFOLK
BURY QUARTER SESSIONS
APRIL 29 1816

WHEREAS disorderly Assemblages of Persons have taken place, and Outrages have been committed in some parts of the Division of Bury St. Edmunds : The Magistrates present at the above session do hereby signify their determination to take prompt and effectual measures to put a stop to all such assemblages, and to bring to justice all persons who are found offending against the peace.

And the Magistrates will, in their respective districts, take such measures for strengthening the hands of the civil power, as shall seem necessary to preserve the peace therein.

BY ORDER

(Essex) were destroyed between eleven and twelve o'clock the following night.[32] At Clare, farm buildings belonging to John Shelton and a poor man's cottage were burnt, and threshing tackle was ceremoniously destroyed at nearby Stoke-by-Clare,[33] a crime which was carried out during daytime with no attempt at secrecy, and for which Mary Jackson and seven men were imprisoned.[34] At Stanningfield farm, outbuildings were fired,[35] and somewhat earlier office buildings belonging to a Mr. Royal of St. Michael's Colsany suffered the same fate. Haulm stacks belonging to a farmer named Harvey were burnt at Hartest on the 6th, and more belonging to Turner at Brockford four days later. Practically every farmer who could do so was by this time putting a round-the-clock guard on his possessions like Major Marrie, but great consternation was caused at Lawshall when a barn full of wheat was set alight on a Sunday during divine service when the vigil was relaxed.[36] For this crime James Pleasants, a thirteen-year-old lad, was sent for trial and was sentenced to death alongside Joseph Bugg—although he was reprieved later. At Needham Market on the 7th the first attack on a flour mill took place when a mob of over 100 assembled outside Hayward's premises and broke the windows.[37] They, however, were persuaded to disperse without doing any further damage.

In Cambridgeshire there was a demonstration demanding lower prices at Haverhill on the 15th and a more serious incident on 7th May at Swaffham Bulbeck, the little place at which celebrations for the victory over the Property Tax had been so extreme. A crowd of fifty or more, led by William Hullier (reported in the newspapers as Ullyar) and James Thompson, both labourers from Swaffham, met and began to demand higher wages. They and four other labourers were eventually charged with riotous assembly at the Cambridge Quarter Sessions, but there was not enough evidence to convict. There was plenty of evidence to find them guilty of assaulting William Manning, another labourer, however, who had refused to join them in demonstrating. Manning was the first of many "blacklegs" to be treated in this way and his assailants received sentences ranging from three to six months. It might be of interest to note that the people who went bail for Thompson and Hullier were John Miller, cordwainer, and Henry Bentley of Bottisham, a cooper.[38]

The incidents described so far all took place in small country villages or market towns. On the 14th May, however, riots took place in the important centre of Bury St. Edmunds, a town of 8,000 or more inhabitants. The Duke of Grafton had, as early as the 1st May, circularised the magistrates in Suffolk, on instructions from Lord Sidmouth (who was obviously alarmed by Marrie's letters),[39] urging them to take firm action and employ police help from London if necessary.[40] The first object of attack by "diabolical incendiaries" were outhouses in Southgate Street, the property of Robert Gooday.[41] The next day the mob proceeded to the house of Mr. Wales, a hosier, where they demanded "that he should give up a machine called a spinning jenny".[42] Some considerable damage was done, but Charles Bromfield and the magistrates, with the aid of the West Suffolk Militia, were successful in dispersing the crowd and making a number of arrests.[43] The following day, 200 special constables were sworn in, nightly patrols started, an all-night guard put on Wales' premises and eventually troops moved in. Bury ceased to be a major source of trouble, although there were riots there spread over three or four days. The next serious incidents occurred in Brandon on the 16th, obviously inspired by what had gone on in Bury and the surrounding villages.

Newspaper reports of the incidents at Brandon were both exaggerated in their accounts of the violence and incorrect in detail. It is possible, however, from the briefs prepared for the Treasury solicitors and the correspondence that took place between the Home Office and people like Marrie and Grafton, to build up a comprehensive account of the events of those fateful days. Brandon at the time had a population of about 1,200[44] and industry seems to have consisted of the making of gun flints and very little else.[45]

A crowd of about 200 people, mainly women and boys, assembled in a riotous mood in the market place at Brandon at about four o'clock in the afternoon of Thursday, 16th May.[46] Mr. Burch and J. Moseley, two magistrates who were at the latter's home at Toft's Hall, some five miles away over the border in Norfolk, were sent for by frightened constables unable to quieten the crowd. They arrived during the early evening and immediately proceeded to the *Chequers Inn*. They sent out for a number of people—some twenty-five in all—like Matthew Burrell, the proprietor of the *White Hart Inn*, whom they swore in as special constables. Burch then went out to address the crowd. He asked them what they wanted and they replied, *"Cheap Bread, a Cheap Loaf and Provisions Cheaper"*. By this time they were in an ugly mood, amusing themselves by breaking the windows of a house belonging to a Mrs. Brewster, and were being urged by Henry Spendlove, a labourer who was armed with a stick, to even greater deeds of violence. Burrell and Thomas Willett, a butcher who was an object of great hatred to the crowd, went out to make some arrests but thought better of it and returned to *The Chequers* amidst a hail of stones. Burch then told the crowd that, unless they dispersed, he would have to read the Riot Act, and sent the clerk for "the volume of Buries Justice which contains the proclamation directed by the Riot Act". This had the desired effect and the crowd, which had dwindled to between thirty and forty, dispersed quietly after hearing Burch read his piece at about a quarter to eleven.

The magistrates by this time had lost their nerve and Moseley sent to the Commanding officer of some Dragoons stationed at Thetford, five or six miles away, "where a riot had lately been".[47] Lieutenant Stephen Goodenough and eleven men of the First Royal Dragoons arrived in Brandon between two and three o'clock on the morning of 17th May to find the town perfectly quiet. Burch and Moseley, who was later quite unjustly accused of running away,[48] went home during the night.

The following day, John Kendle, a deputy overseer, met, on the bridge over the river, a crowd of about fifty labourers led by Porter Talbot, a labourer armed with a gun "which had a hand-

kerchief tied round the lock". Kendle asked what they wanted
and they replied that Mr. Norman, the miller at Weeting, a half
mile away, "had not kept his word and they were going to pull
his mill down". Kendle argued with them and promised to see
Norman on their behalf, if they would hold their hand. They
agreed and the overseer rode off. When he returned with the
news that Norman had not put his prices up, however, the labourers had already moved into the town.

A crowd had started assembling in the market place at about
nine o'clock that morning. About an hour later some women
came along who announced that their men were following them
but had stopped along the Thetford road to collect sticks. Eventually fifty or more, all armed, and led by William Peverett, a
labourer, marched into the square carrying white and red flags.
Willett, the butcher, who was amongst the crowd, told Peverett
that the parish would let them have flour at 2s. 6d. if they would
disperse, and asked for a deputation to go along with him to meet
the magistrates. Helen Dyer, a married woman, had earlier told
Willett that, although she could not read, she had a paper containing the crowd's demands, which she wanted shown to the
magistrates. On it was written *"Bread or Blood in Brandon this
day"*.

Lieutenant Goodenough at *The Chequers* had sent for Burch,
the magistrate, as soon as the crowd began to assemble. He asked
some of the special constables to go out and arrest Talbot, but
they replied that they were too scared of the mob. When Burch
arrived, the Lieutenant asked for permission to go take some of
the labourers into custody himself, but this the frightened magistrate refused to allow. Instead, he agreed to see the deputation
brought to him by Willett, which included Peverett, Talbot,
Henry Malt, John Crane—all labourers—and William Arnold,
a shoemaker.

Burch asked John Crane why the crowd had assembled again
and what their demands were. Crane replied that "they did not
mean any injury but that he could not live with his large family
as things were, *and they must have flour cheaper*". They also
asked for the military to leave, saying that they did not like the
"Redcoats". The magistrate, by this time scared out of his wits,
appeared ready to make concessions, although Goodenough
warned him that he was acting improperly. He promised that
the military would leave, and saved some face when the Town
Clerk of Thetford opportunely arrived with a message from the

Mayor of that place demanding the return of the troops because
"a mob was assembling there". Goodenough left and Burch, saying that the crowd's demands would be met, arranged a meeting
of "the principal inhabitants" for six o'clock at *The Chequers*.
All this time stones were being thrown outside in the square.

The crowd began to reassemble outside *The Chequers* around
five o'clock and once again women were very prominent and
vociferous. The meeting decided that the poor were to have 2s.
a day allowance and flour at 2s. 6d. a stone as Willett had suggested. Burch announced this decision to the labourers and
agreed to their demand that it be put in writing. Smythe, Burch's
clerk, took the agreements along to the Town Cryer. This was
the first time demands of this kind had been formulated and the
first time that the magistrates had given in. It was to form the
pattern for future incidents.

The crowd announced that they were satisfied with the concessions, and it does not seem to have occurred to any of them
that, having got them by violence, they might not be kept. They
told Burch, however, "We must have beer or worse will come
of it", and in spite of cries from the women saying, "do not give
them any", this was agreed to also—provided they had it in the
Ram Close, a field belonging to *The Ram* Public House. They
drank and danced and eventually went back to the square and
demonstrated their belief in victory by pathetically singing *God
Save the King* and *Rule Britannia* outside *The Chequers*. A
section of them committed some acts of violence, nevertheless,
and the Riot Act was read for the second time. Henry Spendlove
was once again prominent, "forming the men into a rank opposite the windows of the Chequers Inn...". Burrell's windows
were broken, John Ablett was stoned, and between twenty and
thirty people assembled outside Willett's shop and broke his
windows. This was the limit of the damage on Friday, however,
and the crowd "did not commit any more riot or disturbance".

Although they had been promised concessions the day before,
the crowd reassembled on Saturday. This time they were
alleged to have numbered 1,500 and many were armed with
sticks, "the ends of which, to the extent of several inches, were
studded with short iron spikes, sharp at the sides and points".
They also had a flag emblazoned "Bread or Blood" and threatened to march on London. Willett, from whom they had demanded prime joints of beef at 4d. a pound on the earlier days,
was once again the main object of attack, and on this occasion

his shop and house were completely destroyed. The mob then
went off to Halesworth, but there are no reports of trouble either
there or en route. Meanwhile, Willett and the Sheriff of Suffolk
had hastened to London to ask the Home Secretary for military
assistance to quell the rioters.

According to newspaper reports, the magistrates met again on
Monday and confirmed the agreement they had made with the
rioters. *The Courier* said that they "guaranteed the price of
flour at 2s. 6d. per stone, with an advance of wages to 2s. per
head for a fortnight, and unless the millers reduce their prices by
that time, the officers of the parish will purchase their grain at
the cheapest rate, and furnish the poor with provisions at prime
cost". In spite of the fact that troops of the West Norfolk Militia
had gone there from Ipswich, the magistrates at Bury St.
Edmunds agreed to exactly the same terms on the same
day.

The concessions were not simply panic measures, but also
attempts to buy time, and the labourers were left free for over a
week after the riots before being apprehended, even although
troops (in small numbers it must be admitted) were stationed in
Brandon from the Saturday. It is not clear whether the parish
officials kept their part of the bargain to supply cheap corn during that week, but presumably they did. After the show of force
at Ely and elsewhere that finally ended violence on a large scale,
arrests began to be made. Peverett, "a most dangerous character"
who had had a wad of banknotes during the troubles, James
Wiggar, Talbot, Arnold, the shoemaker, and a repentant Henry
Spendlove were committed to gaol on the 28th. Two days later
Mingay Rampling and Helen Dyer, who was described as "a
very good looking young woman", were apprehended and imprisoned, and the following day William Clark and Ann Folkes,
another young lady who was also described to Sidmouth as being
extremely attractive, were similarly charged and held in custody.

These prisoners were among the luckiest of the labourers held
legally responsible for the riots in the summer of 1816. They
were committed to the Suffolk Assizes in August but their cases
were held over.[49] Eight months later they appeared before Baron
Graham on the motion of Mr. Alderson. They were allowed to
withdraw their former plea, change it to guilty and throw themselves on the mercy of the court. By this time the Government
had had its share of blood-letting and the agricultural districts
were relatively quiet. It seemed appropriate for a show of mercy

and the labourers were set free. Graham lectured them on the fact that violence was not a means of bettering their conditions, but said that he was pleased to see young persons guilty of outrage brought to a due sense of their wicked conduct. All nine were discharged upon their own recognizances and ordered to appear and receive judgment if, and when, called upon.[50]

CHAPTER SEVEN

THE BRANDON TROUBLES started on Thursday, 16th May, and were obviously inspired by incidents a few miles away in Bury St. Edmunds. On exactly the same day a much more violent and serious outbreak occurred in Norwich.

That Norwich was a city with a depressed manufacturing population that was both prone to riot and politically conscious has already been mentioned. On Thursday night, around nine o'clock, a mob assembled in the market square and, after some time, began throwing "fire balls". The authorities appear to have been taken completely by surprise. The West Norfolk Militia, in town to be disbanded, were not in their barracks and could not be used to stop trouble developing.[1] The crowd proceeded from the market place "breaking the city lamps on their way" to the New Mills, where people were still at work. The place was broken into, flour taken out and ceremoniously dumped into the river, strewn in the streets, or taken away. For reasons which have not been discovered, they then went to the house of an unpopular Dr. Alderton (or Alderson) whom they knocked down when he remonstrated with them for smashing his windows.[2] At about eleven o'clock a troop of cavalry, directed by Alderman Marsh, emerged from the Town Hall and cleared the streets.

The following day the authorities prepared to resist the inflamed populace. A Court of Mayoralty was held in the Town Hall and the militia were called in from their billets in various parts of the town. A great mob assembled late in the day which showed a decided "disposition to riot". At sunset a captain's guard of the West Norfolk Militia marched into the Town Hall, the Norwich Light Horse Volunteers assembled at *The Swan Inn* and a detachment of the First Royal Dragoons was drawn up in the market square. This display incensed the crowd and Mayor Yallop was forced to read the Riot Act. This was the final straw; the mob began stoning the military who proceeded to clear the streets and make a number of arrests. The Dragoons "galloped up stone steps, rode over posts and rails, and followed wherever the ill-disposed thought themselves most secure". This was a most effective show of force and on Saturday the streets were cleared early and the town kept relatively quiet. Lord Sidmouth in replying to Yallop complimented him on his prompt action.

Whitehall, 20th May 1816.

Sir—I have received your letter of yesterday's date, and I am very happy to learn from it that the preparations made by yourself and the other magistrates for checking any tumult or riot have had the effect of preventing further outrages on the part of the ill-disposed. I beg you will accept my thanks for your communication. Should these outrages be renewed, I shall hope to hear from you on the subject.

I am, Sir
Your most obedient humble servant
SIDMOUTH

The Worshipful Mayor of Norwich.

On Monday, 20th May, a number of persons were brought before the magistrates and committed to gaol or bound over to appear later, but there was still a strong "disposition to riot" in the city. Things were kept in control until a week or so later, when great confusion ensued "in consequence of verbal notices given by the banks that no old shillings and sixpences would be received by them".[3] Fears were expressed about what might happen on the following Saturday, and "the lower orders", according to Yallop, were once again on the verge of rioting.[4] Prompt action by him again prevented disaster, when he ordered the overseers to accept and change any silver the poor might bring to them.

The trials of the prisoners charged with offences in Norwich took place at the Midsummer Sessions in that city. Once again they were fortunate: no true bill was found against Hardy Sheppard, and Robert Hatton the younger, charged with misdemeanour and riotous assembly on the 17th, when he was alleged to have used fireballs against the cavalry, was sentenced to three months.[5] Later in the year, recompense was made to the people whose property had been damaged in May.

"The several persons whose windows, &c., were broken in May last," it was reported in *The Norwich Mercury* (30th November), "were within these few days paid by the Chief Constable the amount of their respective damages, in the whole about £500, thereby causing the poor rates to be 6d. in the pound more last quarter than they otherwise would have been."

Norwich was quiet by the 21st May, but incidents had meanwhile occurred elsewhere in Norfolk. At Hockham, on the previous Sunday, a crowd of nearly 100 had assembled to destroy a threshing machine belonging to William Burlingham. He had let it out to Mr. Wells, a farmer at Hockham, and the mob had dragged it off the land and broken it. A Mr. Cooper, a defence lawyer, ingeniously suggested that the labourers eventually tried for the offences were simply trying to clear an obstruction and inadvertently damaged it in the process, but to little avail. Peter Palmer (sixty-three) and his son of the same name were given three months' imprisonment at the Norfolk Quarter Sessions. John Abery, or Abry, and James Bailey received a year each.[6]

Hockham is very close to an area where trouble threatened, but never got out of hand. The threatening letter found at Ashill has already been quoted and there are a number of letters from the Reverend Benjamin Barker of Caston, near Watton, in the Home Office correspondence which show that the area in which he lived was disaffected. "There is a great ferment in this whole neighbourhood," he told Sidmouth on the 21st May, "and some mischief has already been done." He spent six hours, he said, arguing with a crowd at Rockland and succeeded in persuading them not to riot. During all this, he said, "I found many causes of very great distress". The crowd had been armed and had intended to march to other parishes. He also said that the "bad dispositions" extended beyond the "lower orders" but did not say whether any from this higher class were present in the mob. Barker also made it quite clear that what had happened at Bury and elsewhere influenced the labourers, when he concluded a letter by saying that "From fear, ignorance or mistaken benevolence, promises which cannot be performed, have in several places been made to the people—the news is spread around in all directions. . .". For his part in calming his area, Sidmouth recommended Barker to the Lord Lieutenant as a suitable person to become a magistrate.[7]

There was also an incident at Stoke Ferry on the 17th May, when George Killengrey set fire to premises belonging to H. Dynes of that place. A few days later trouble occurred at Mundford, where, owing to the "early attention and activity of A. J. Moseley, Esq., [the man charged with running away from Brandon], the Swaffham Cavalry, under Captains Hammond and Thyssen, were mustered". The crowd was "armed with bludgeons, &c.," and the Riot Act was read. The troops patrolled

the street and "entire order was the consequence".[8] At Dickleburgh, some miles away from the usual trouble area, there was
a blaze on Saturday, 18th May, of which "strong suspicions
[were] entertained of it being maliciously set on fire".[9]

With the exception of the stoning of the hated Yeomanry at
Norwich, and something similar, though less serious, at Brandon,
the incidents reported so far were marked by the absence of
attacks on persons. Real violence, however, appeared in the little
village of Hockwold-cum-Wilton, just over the border in Norfolk, on the 17th May. Prosecution briefs were prepared for the
Treasury Solicitors to proceed against a number of labourers for
incidents there and at Feltwell, a few miles away, and it is mainly
from these that the following description is built up.[10]

A crowd of almost 100 assembled in Hockwold, which, incidentally, was in the process of being enclosed (Act passed 1814,
award announced 1818), on Friday, the 17th May, "and did
make Noise, Riot, Rout, Tumult and Disturbance" for over six
hours. They gathered early outside the house of the Reverend
William Newcombe, where, apparently, they were resisted by
James Stark, a carpenter from Stoke Ferry. Stark was confronted by John Howers, one of the labourers who "did beat,
bruise, wound and ill-treat him so that his life was greatly
despaired of", and then forced him to go with the crowd into the
Vicar's house. It is not clear whether Newcombe was robbed
but later the crowd, led by Howers, Thomas Newton and another labourer named Wilton, went along and demanded beer
from a Mrs. Grace Rolfe, who was forced to part with two
quarts.

On the following day, the 18th, trouble broke out in Feltwell,
another place which had just been enclosed (Act 1813, award
1815). A crowd began to assemble at six in the morning, led by
Jeremiah Lawrence, Richard Browne and Thomas Pleasance,
all labourers from the village, and John Cracknell, described as
a "yeoman" of the same place. They went on a tour of the
village, armed with pitchforks, demanding money from the
local farmers. At the house of William Nurse, his wife was forced
to agree to let them drink beer to be credited to her in each of
the four local public houses. John Flowers, when approached,
said "they should have no Pound Bill of him", but when told
by the crowd that "Mr. Siggar (?) had given them 10s. and
Mrs. Clough £6", replied "I do not wish to be singular, you
may take 10s. worth of beer at *The Cock*". Flowers seems to have

been remarkably brave and polite, although not brave enough
to persist in refusing the crowd's demands, as he said he originally intended.

During the afternoon, the Feltwell labourers destroyed the
dams that had been built across some nearby land drains, went
"to Mr. Denton's land and there threw down part of a fence",
and then went to confront Mr. Willett, a shopkeeper. Cracknell
was spokesman. He took off his hat and said, "I hope, sir, you
will please to give us something".[11] Willett asked how much
Thomas Fuller had given them and was told £1. Willett agreed
to give this amount and Cracknell seemed disposed to accept,
but his colleagues demanded, and got, an extra pound. They
then forced George Linnard, a labourer and apparently a "black-
leg", to go with them to *The Bell* where they relieved him of a
shilling and sent him on his way. The rest of the evening was
spent carousing, according to Mrs. Nurse who eventually got a
bill for 30s. for beer consumed at *The Bell*, *The Chequers* and
The Cock.

Cracknell, Lawrence and Pleasance were tried for assaulting
Thomas Willett, at the Norfolk and Norwich Assizes in August.
Under cross-examination Willett said that cutting the dam was
the crowd's prime object, and defending counsel cleverly con-
tended that the first pound the shopkeeper handed over was in
payment for the destruction. This got the trio acquitted and they,
unlike some of the Ely rioters, were not re-charged. Other indictments against Browne and Lawrence were not proceeded
with. All were ordered to find sureties for good behaviour and
then discharged.[12]

The area near Feltwell was quiet on Sunday. On Monday,
20th May, however, while Hardy Sheppard and the others were
appearing in court at Norwich, really serious rioting broke out
in Downham Market and the day ended with that town in a
state of chaos. It was general throughout the area for magistrates
and overseers to hold weekly meetings, usually on a Monday,
and on that day the representatives of the Hundred and Half of
Clacklose were meeting in Downham. The labourers set out to
confront them.[13]

At some time between seven and eight o'clock, a crowd of
about sixty began to gather in the little village of Southerey, a
few miles from Feltwell. Among them, some who "displayed
some military knowledge" began to press the fainter hearts in
the village into joining them. James Galley, a labourer, was

spokesman and he led them to Robert Martin's farm, where labourers were forced to unyoke their horses and join the crowd. A little later they called at the unpopular John Benton's farm and compelled another three men to leave their work. John Stern, a labourer, threatened to break open the barn, but Benton was armed, and the crowd went off towards Downham Market, led by John Bowers blowing a horn. They arrived at Denver at about ten o'clock and pressed more men into their ranks. Stern threatened they would hang anyone who persisted in refusing to join them, and the crowd was in an ugly mood. Sarah More, a labouring woman from Hilgay, was heard to say they wanted "Bread or Blood".

Robert Martin, the Southerey farmer, had ridden ahead of the crowd and called on Mr. Dering, a local magistrate, warning him that several hundreds of angry labourers were approaching Downham Market. Dering first of all asked what their demands were, then sent to Captain Lee, who was about nine miles away, asking him to assemble the Upwell Yeomanry Cavalry. He then went into town and tried to enrol the populace as special constables, but "To his great disappointment he found his neighbours little disposed to exert themselves at that period".[14] John Balding, an overseer of the poor, went out to meet the crowd.

Balding met the crowd on the outskirts of the town and asked them what they were about. He was told that they intended to see the magistrates and heard some complaints from certain labourers that they were being forced to demonstrate against their will. When the labourers began breaking into Simpson's bread shop and distributing the loaves, he went back to report to the magistrates meeting at *The Crown Inn*. He stayed there until the crowd assembled outside, in the market place, at twelve o'clock. En route they had broken into a shop belonging to John Parkinson, whose wife had locked the place and fled in panic. Scores of labourers from Downham had joined them and one report put their numbers as high as 1,500. Women were prominent amongst them, Frances Porter in particular. They broke down Parkinson's door and stole and distributed loaves of bread and 140 lbs. of flour. They also practically denuded the shop of sheeting, shoes, hats, umbrellas and so on. Only 6s. in cash was taken, but the whole of the loot was valued at over £18. Much of it was taken back later in the day, although some of it was sold. Another crowd, led by William Bell, Charles Nelson, Spencer Rayner and Hannah Jarvis, robbed George

Thomas of four to five gallons of beer. As yet, however, things had not got completely out of hand and a courageous drover named Richard Gamble forced his way into Thomas's house, locked the cellar doors and turned the mob away.

A constable on duty outside *The Crown* took a message to the magistrates and overseers saying that the Southerey people wanted to talk to them. By this time the magistrates had determined to make some concessions and a deputation of eight labourers was invited in. They stated terms exactly like those agreed to at Brandon and Bury and said they wanted work and 2s. a day. They were then asked to go into another room while their demands were considered. When they returned, they were told that "the circumstances of produce being so much lowered in value the Farmers and others could not afford to grant what they wished", but that they agreed to allow 2s. a day and to supply flour at 2s. 6d. per stone "for those that had large families". This led to a tremendous argument, during which the magistrates and overseers displayed considerable courage, refusing to move from their original offer to make their concessions applicable to everyone, as at Brandon. John Bowers, the labourer, was particularly violent towards Robert Scale, an overseer, who told him, "You seem to be very forward with that large stick in your hand, but I am not to be intimidated by that". Bowers replied, "Yes, here's my stick, it never did anybody any harm yet—whatever it might do".

The magistrates followed the deputation outside into the square and addressed the crowd, asking them to go away. They were in no mood to disperse when they heard of the magistrates' stand, however, and began demanding the release of a gang of poachers who had recently been imprisoned in the town. Stones were thrown and the J.P.s were forced back into *The Crown*, followed by the crowd. Hare and Pratt escaped, but Dering was chased and eventually found refuge by hiding in the garden of Mr. Wales, the apothecary—whose house (according to one report) was broken up by labourers who were seeking the unfortunate magistrate. Another part of the crowd stayed inside *The Crown*, which they tore apart. They took flour and other eatables and made Samuel Johnson, the publican, supply them with fifteen gallons of beer, all of which they consumed during the afternoon. Among those active here was Sindall, the rioter eventually shot at Littleport, and the only person known to have been involved at more than one place in the May riots.

The afternoon of Monday, 20th May, was given over to plunder and rioting in Downham—albeit here, as elsewhere, little violence was done to individuals (although Dering would have been in trouble had he been found). By this time Daniel Harwood, thirty-two, a native of Gooderstone, who was self-employed doing contract work with his waggon and team for farmers "as is the custom in that part of the country where he resided, near Downham", and Thomas Thody, twenty-two, born at St. Neots, a married man with two children and then living at Nacton, had become prominent as leaders of the crowd. Thody was one of those who had imbibed at the landlord's expense at *The Crown*.

One of the first objects of attack during the afternoon was William Baldwin's flour mill. Thody and Harwood led a crowd to the mill where they relieved William Spinks, a millhand, of the key. Charles Nelson opened the door and the crowd rushed in and helped themselves, distributing, according to Baldwin, flour and seventy bushels of meal to the value of £35 10s. 0d. Elizabeth King and Nelson then robbed Mary Wyer of twenty loaves of bread and John Stern procured 12 lbs. of cheese which he took to *The Crown* and distributed among his friends. Hannah Jarvis led an attack on Stimson's shop where she cut up some loin of beef and distributed it amongst the rioters. From there she and Amelia Lightharness took a crowd to the shop of Francis Wiseman, a pork butcher. Amelia was heard to say "Here my boys, this is the place for good pork" and the crowd denuded the place, taking 250 lbs. of meat, valued at £9. Zachariah Stebbing, a gardener, said that he noticed William Bell, the yeoman, particularly active. "I noticed Bell," he said, "and thought that a man like him who *kept a team of horses of his own* should rob his neighbour." From Wiseman's, the crowd went to Samuel Bolton's shop. Bolton had already been forced earlier to give up all his cooked meats and was surprised when the mob called on him again late in the afternoon. He slammed the door and ran to get his guns, but William Fendyke, Harwood and Thody smashed the door in and the crowd helped themselves. Bolton said that Lightharness, Lucy Rumbelow and Anne Fuller were very prominent. Another section of the crowd went off to try to liberate the poachers.

At about five o'clock Captain Lee arrived with some men of the Clacklose Yeomanry Cavalry. Dering, still hiding in the chemist's garden, heard the troops and climbed over a wall to join them. He led them on horseback to the market place and there read the Riot Act. As he finished, the part of the crowd which had tried to release the poachers returned and the market place was once again turned into a battleground. Stones were thrown at the hated yeomanry,[15] who retaliated by hitting out with the flats of their swords. Eventually the crowd dispersed although, according to John Lister, one of the cavalrymen, there were still troubles as late as seven o'clock. The troops and the special constables (seventy had enrolled after the cavalry arrived!) searched the public houses and imprisoned six or seven labourers. Lord Suffield told Sidmouth that, but for the arrival of Captain Lee, Dering's house would have been in flames.[16]

The following day a crowd in Southerey, led by Stern, John Neal and Hardy, waited upon Robert Martin. They told the farmer that they wanted the release of their colleagues who had been arrested the day before, and sent him off to confer with the magistrates in Downham Market, while they set out to do the journey on foot. More labourers joined them at Hilgay and on this occasion they were a much more orderly and formidable force than before. William Hardy seems to have been in charge and he had drilled them in how to meet a cavalry charge.[17] Added to the pitchforks and fork irons were now thirty to forty guns, some of which had been stolen. James Goat and John Bell for instance took powder and shot from Isaac Ashley and Robert Bond, shopkeepers at Hilgay, during a break there. Bell told Ashley that what they took would be paid for—"after they had met the soldiers".

In Downham Market, Martin saw Dering and Pratt, the magistrates, and told them what demands had been made. They arranged for the Southerey labourers to be released and then went out to meet the crowd. En route from Southerey, the mob grew to about 500 in number, some of whom were pressed into joining. (Joseph Gallaway, for instance, who had been working at Modney Bridge was forced by Gamaliel Porter to march at the point of a gun.)

Martin and Dering told the crowd that the Southerey labourers had been released and the Southerey men seemed satisfied. "The Hilgay men however forced them forward and said they should not return unless their men were liberated also." Dering and Pratt conferred and agreed to release all the prisoners (it is not clear whether this included the poachers).

They told this to the crowd, who expressed their satisfaction and dispersed to their villages. *The Star* expressed a general opinion of the magistrates' behaviour in a report on the 25th May.

The inhabitants were armed under the directions of the Magistrates;—[and] marched out, with the cavalry, to meet the rioters, who were also armed;—and then ensued, what?—an agreement, that the latter should have an advance of wages, and that the persons already taken should be allowed to return to their homes! —We hope there is an error in the statement; but, as something of that sort has occurred elsewhere, we cannot let the report of such a compromise pass, without saying, that this mode of suppressing tumults is that, which of all others is sure to multiply them. . . . Any concession, if it be but the gift of a turnip, made to a body of men unlawfully in arms, is a matter of danger to society, and it is not unreasonable to impute this outrage against Downham to the success of a similar one at Brandon.[18]

The day following the amnesty, the better-known riots broke out in Littleport, a few miles to the south of Southerey! It might be as well, however, before describing these incidents, to conclude the story of Downham Market.

Dering rode off to London on the Tuesday evening and reported to the Secretary of State's office where he asked for military aid, the Upwell Cavalry having returned home after the agreement with the labourers. On the Friday (after the Littleport riots had been forcibly put down) there was a scare in Downham Market. Another visit was expected from the Southerey labourers because the concessions the magistrates had agreed to on Monday had not been kept. It is said that the labourers demanded an allowance of 2s. a day for the two days they had spent rioting. By this time it must have been perfectly clear from what had happened at Ely and Littleport that the concessions would not be kept, and that the full force of the law would descend upon those responsible for the riots. Nevertheless, there was some violence and the Yeomanry were sent for again. Four troops arrived and during the early evening guns were seized and the rioters released on Tuesday were again taken into custody. Seven were committed for trial on the Saturday and more were brought in over the weekend.

In August, labourers, both male and female, appeared before the Judge at the Norfolk and Norwich Assizes charged with riots at Hilgay, Southerey and Downham Market. Nine men and six women were sentenced to death, no true bills were found against one man and one woman, seven people were bound over to keep the peace and appear at the next Assizes, if called, and John Stern was given seven years' transportation for riotous conduct. Of those sentenced to death only Thomas Thody and Daniel Harwood were left for execution, the others being transported. Charles Nelson and John Pearson, for instance, sailed in *The Shipley* from Portsmouth for New South Wales on the 20th October 1816; Amelia Lightharness and Hannah Jarvis left in *The Friendship* for the same destination in June of the following year.[19]

Attempts were made to save the two men sentenced to death. There is a pathetic petition on behalf of Harwood in the Home Office papers signed by his father saying that, as his son was christened Dan and not Daniel, he had been wrongly charged. The people of Downham Market also asked for leniency, maintaining that the two were led astray by "the fatal example of the people of Southerey who came with many others into Downham to lay their complaints before the Magistrates" and "the bad women of the place". The Downham petition was signed by four of the prosecutors, three overseers, two churchwardens and over seventy townspeople,[20] but it had no effect.

Harwood and Thody, along with Thomas Moy, condemned to death for sheep stealing, were executed in public in Norwich on 31st August 1816. The executions always attracted huge crowds and certain superstitious practices had grown up around them.[21] The *Norwich Mercury* described the dispatch of the unhappy trio at length.[22]

On Saturday last were executed on the Castle Hill, Thomas Moy, for sheep stealing, and Thomas Thody and Daniel Harwood, for rioting at Downham. They were all of them men of honest and reputable connections, and were brought to their untimely end by sabbath-breaking—by bad company of both sexes—by occasional intoxication, when in their power—and by following a multitude to do evil. As far as their time permitted, they endeavoured to atone for their former neglect of their duty to God, by assiduously employing themselves in devotional exercises, and there is reason to think that, had their lives been spared, they would have been better men, better subjects, and better Christians; but the prevalence and danger of the crimes for which their lives were forfeited and the necessity of making severe examples to deter others from similar crimes, rendered all applications in their favour to the higher powers fruitless. Their behaviour since they were left for execution, was meek and contrite; and they passed their weary hours in reading the Scriptures, in fervent prayer, and in attentively listening to the terms of salvation held out by the Saviour to truly penitent sinners. Having taken a last farewell of their relatives and friends, and an affecting leave of their fellow prisoners, and after being indulged in waiting till the last moment, in the forlorn hope of reprieve, they proceeded to the place of execution.—When the prayers appropriated to the solemn occasion were concluded, they submitted, with manly resignation, to the awful preparations for death. Harwood was first fixed to the fatal tree. Thody was the next sufferer, and he suffered indeed, as far as related to mental suffering : he had hitherto conducted himself with patient fortitude, and with a steady step had ascended the scaffold; but, when the rope was placed on his neck, the remembrance of his wife and children, whom he loudly called upon and deplored, overwhelmed his mind, and with agonizing screams he would have fallen in a fit, had he not been supported by the exhortations of the Ordinary and of his fellow-sufferers, and by the soothing attentions of those around him, he recovered soon from his fainting state, and stood up firmly while the executioner performed his office upon him and Moy, who was the last tied up. The raised part of the platform immediately fell, and they died with some convulsive struggles, in which Moy appeared to be the longest sufferer. No malefactors ever expired with greater sympathy from the immense multitude, which covered the whole surface of the hill adjoining the place of execution.— Thomas Moy, aged 32, was born at Guestwick in Norfolk, and has left a wife and seven young children. The pressure of the times had involved him in great distress; and he had undertaken to hire a farm of considerable extent at Binham, to which his circumstances were by no means equal. His relations are respectable, and the crime for which he suffered was the only one which brought him under the sentence of the law.—Daniel Harwood, aged 32, was a native of Gooderstone, in Norfolk, unmarried, and pursued an agricultural mode of life, by occasionally working with his waggon and team in jobs for farmers, as is the custom, in that part of the country where he resided, near Downham. This wandering manner of life led him into bad company, and together with a neglect of his religious duties, at length involved him in the riots which brought him to his untimely end.—Thomas Thody, aged 22, was born at St. Neots, in Huntingdonshire, and has resided several years at Necton, [sic] in Norfolk, where his father was coachman to the late Mr. Mason. He has left a wife and two small children.

CHAPTER EIGHT

THE INCIDENTS INVOLVING the Southerey labourers took place on the 20th and 21st May. Having secured the release of their friends, they returned to their village in high spirits and sent out messengers to nearby villages to spread the news of their victory over the magistrates. Among those told were the labourers of Littleport, a few miles away. They, according to one of the solicitors who drew up a statement of the events of the 22nd, 23rd and 24th May, "lost no time in asserting *their* Rights (as they audaciously expressed themselves)".[1] The "Norfolk Banditti", he said, had "succeeded too well" at Downham Market.

The labourers at Littleport met in *The Globe* public house on the evening of 22nd May for a Benefit Club meeting, and, without doubt, the recent incidents at Bury, Brandon, and Downham Market, were discussed by the fifty or sixty people present. According to Johnson, they were expecting the men from Southerey. Undoubtedly, the usual amount of drinking went on, and, when it was realised that their neighbours were not joining them, they issued forth from *The Globe* and made straight for the house of the Rev. John Vachell, the vicar of Littleport, an extremely unpopular magistrate.

Vachell was at home when the crowd called. He was told that the labourers wanted work and bread and he was asked to accompany them to a parley with the farmers. Vachell agreed to do this and the crowd met the farmers in the churchyard. Prominent among the latter was Henry Martin who acted as spokesman and who was described as "a principal Farmer in the Parish against whom some of them (the labourers) had imbibed an animosity", and elsewhere as someone who was obnoxious "because of his conduct in the affairs of the parish". (He was an overseer of the poor in 1814.) Martin promised the crowd "2s. per day and flour at 2s. 6d. per stone", exactly the same terms, he said, that he had heard the Southerey people had been awarded. By this time windows were being broken nearby and Martin said that "I was then advised to go home—and did so".

A crowd led by a man blowing a horn had broken away from those negotiating with the farmers and begun rioting and robbing on a scale not seen at Brandon, Bury or Downham Market. An un-dated though probably unreliable confession signed by Henry Benson exists in the Public Record Office which may refer to Wednesday, 22nd May. If it does, it would seem that some labourers from Southerey *might* have joined the mob by then—although none were charged with offences at Littleport. It is headed "Voluntary Confession of Henry Benson", who, it goes on,

says that Thomas Porter of Southerey is the first man who came to Littleport—I met him going and asked him what he was going to do—he said he was going to cause a riot at Littleport to attack Downham and get flour cheaper. I saw him coming back again towards Brandon Creek—Southerey people met him—when he got to Brandon Creek he said to Clark and Crick (?) and John Porter that if they would not go he would take a cudgel and knock their Brains out—Neal and Clark came to my farm and made my son in law John Porter go—Brandon Creek people and Porter returned same day—Little Easey was the first man who blew the Horn. I heard Mark Benton say that they were determined not to say who blew the Horn they would die first

> The X Mark of Henry Benson.

Taken before H. Bate Dudley.

One of the first objects of attack was a grocer's shop kept by Stephen and Mary Wiles. The windows were broken and Mrs. Wiles said that the crowd demanded that she should hand over £10. She offered £1 and they then settled for a bank token worth 1s. 6d. [*sic*]. Aaron Chevell (described usually as a labourer, but in one brief as a tailor), then relieved Stephen Wiles of £8 and the crowd set out for the house of John Mobbs, who was knocked down and robbed by John Easey of £3 "and one loaf of bread worth 1s.".

From John Mobbs' house the crowd went to that of Josiah Dewey, a retired farmer of over seventy years of age. Aaron Chevell said to the old man, "Now if you will give me a £1 note I will go away", but Dewey foolishly said he did not have one. Chevell told the mob to "Go it". "Little" Easey and Richard Jessop knocked the old man down and about fifty labourers forced their way into the house. Mrs. Dewey was told to go off and borrow £1 for them while her husband was held a prisoner. When she returned and handed the money over she found her house being cleared of anything at all valuable, including sheets, table cloths, stockings, a watch, gowns and a cleaver, which Thomas South appropriated and used with considerable effect later on. The crowd also found 100 guineas and a promissory note which they took.

The success at Dewey's prompted the labourers to go to practically all the farmers and shopkeepers in Littleport, demanding money. Robert Crabbe took £1 from Henry Tansley, and Jarvis Cranwell and Thomas Sindall demanded a contribution from John Cutlack junior. Cutlack offered £3, but this was refused and he had to give £5, along with "a piece of paper containing a Minute of his having paid the Money to Sindall". William Beamiss senior, the shoemaker, took £1 from Thomas Waddelow and his son took more from Robert Cheesewright. Later he and Chevell went to Tansley again. Chevell, who was one of Tansley's tenants, anounced "I am at the head of the Mob", and Beamiss told the crowd "that he was cashier" and that "the old fellow [Tansley] has got the money, let us lug it out". The farmer handed over another £2. George Kidd was also visited twice, Thomas South deciding that the 6s. he had given the first time was not enough. South, wielding his cleaver, was also mainly responsible for robbing Robert Whitworth, a farmer, and entering the house of Mrs. Elizabeth Little and taking 10s. Aaron Chevell also took £1 4s. od. from George Aldis, a surgeon, and returned later to enquire whether or not the note was a good one! Henry Luddington, a magistrate, was one of the few people spared, he having persuaded Beamiss to leave his house alone.[2]

At about nine o'clock the labourers decided to bring some organisation into the proceedings and Aaron Chevell led a group to the house of Rayner Brassett, a baker and flour dealer who was later charged with rioting, but turned Crown witness. Brassett was asked for a pen and paper to put down an account of how much they had obtained, and then the question arose of who was to be treasurer. Taylor, a labourer who appears quite often in the story yet who was never charged, was asked but declined. "Chevell then said let me hold it but the others replied no if Chevell has it we shall never get it again. Brassett shall hold it." The money, some £25, to which more was added during the evening (what happened to Dewey's 100 guineas is unknown), was put into a handkerchief and handed over to Mrs. Brassett. The crowd left to continue levying and wrecking, saying they would call back the following day.

Thomas South, William Dann and Robert Crabbe then led an

attack upon the house of Robert Speechley "a very feeble and harmless character of upwards of 71 years of age". South, brandishing his cleaver, told the people in the house that "he would serve them as he had served Dewey and not leave them a chair to sit upon". He took £2 12s. 0d. from Sarah Butcher, a servant, and William Dann, who was "in liquor", took £1 from Thomas Cheesewright, who had gone into the house after being robbed in the street by William Beamiss. The place was then systematically broken up and glassware worth £20, twenty ounces of silver, linen and a quantity of money were taken.

By this time the labourers had tasted success and from Speechley's they set out to hunt the unpopular Henry Martin. He lived with his grandparent, Mrs. Rebecca Waddelow, a shopkeeper, and had in fact hidden in the house, although he made his escape as soon as he heard the crowd approaching, shouting for his blood. Joseph Easey led the mob and Mrs. Waddelow, who was said to be "remarkable (70–80 years) for Piety, Charity and Simplicity of character", sent out her servant, "Little" Sallis, to negotiate with him. Sallis offered Easey £5 to go away but this was refused, Easey saying that he would "have Martin". Richard Jessop was also asked to take the cash, but he, too, refused, "for Martin he would have". The crowd, in which John Walker bearing "an ensign" was prominent, then smashed their way into the house.

Inside the house the crowd found Mary Cutlack, who was robbed of £3, and William, the brother of Henry Martin. Thomas South, who one report said was a servant of Henry's "whom he would doubtlessly have murdered had he met him . . . sought to gratify his disappointed malice upon the Prosecutor (William)". South aimed a blow with his cleaver but missed and the farmer made his escape, along with William Gillett, who had been beaten and said he left "through fear". Thomas Gotobed, who was also anxious to settle with Martin, and others then proceeded to search the house and, not finding their prey, chopped up every piece of furniture they could lay their hands upon. They then "cleared the shop" of food and clothing worth some £50, and George Crow took about £6 in notes. Only one known member of the crowd was not from Littleport. This was Thomas Edgerley, a waterman from Ramsey, who had been working on a gang of lighters that were lying near Littleport bridge. He had joined the rioters and had taken tea and cloth worth £10 from Waddelow's shop, which he kept and eventually sold.

Henry Martin had managed to get away from the crowd and had met Hugh Robert Evans, a local solicitor and clerk to the magistrates of Ely. The two of them tried to get away from Littleport in a post chaise, but were stopped by William Beamiss, John Hunt and a few others, who demanded money. Evans was relieved of 14s. and Martin, who kept in the shadows and concealed his real identity, parted with 4s. 6d. This was one of the offences chosen to go before the Judges at the Special Assizes, and one of the few that Beamiss was found not guilty of.

The crowd returned to the Rev. Vachell's house at about eleven o'clock. First of all they demanded money and beer. Two pounds were handed over and they were told they could have a barrel, but Isaac Harley, who was armed with a gun, said this was not enough and threatened to shoot the Vicar and his gardener. Vachell made the mistake of brandishing a pistol and the infuriated crowd, knocking him aside, forced their way into the house. Mr. and Mrs. Vachell and their daughter, "an amicable and interesting young lady in extremely ill-health", managed to make their escape leaving the house to the mercies of the mob. The place was broken up and everything of value was taken, including twenty pounds of flour, silver spoons, "the 5th volume of the Botanical Magazine, a framed portrait of Philip Metcalfe, Esq., and a Bell pull . . ." which were discovered in the house of Elizabeth Watson.

Vachell eventually sued the Hundred of Ely under the Act 1st. George I (the Riot Act) to recover the damages sustained by him and was awarded £708 9s. od.[3] The decision did not go unchallenged and there were numerous complaints about the assessments levied on the various districts. One correspondent of the *Bury Post* pointed out that the tiny hamlet of Welche's Dam was assessed six times higher than the Dean and Theological College in Ely, which had a revenue of £10,000–£12,000 a year.[4] Another correspondent pointed out that Flanders Hopkin, one of the people tried for rioting, who earned 10s.–12s. a week, was assessed at 12s. 6d. while the Dean and Prebends were assessed at 5s. each.[5] Yet a third drew attention to the fact that Bate Dudley, a Prebend who will appear in the story later, was expected to pay only the same amount as the gardener at the College, and that many tradesmen were assessed at £5— or as much as the whole college or "twenty times more than each

individual therein".[6] Vachell, it was reported in March, was to
"resist the rate which had been imposed upon him [sic], in
common with the other inhabitants of the Hundred and College
of Ely, to make compensation to him for the injury he sustained
by the late riots at Littleport—Mr. V's assessment amounts to as
nearly as possible five times the amount of the aggregate sum at
which the whole College has been charged".[7] In the same month
there was a report that a Mr. Vipan, of Welche's Dam, had
replevied the stock which had been distrained for Vachell's rate,
and that the case might go to the King's Bench.[8]

After wrecking Vachell's house, the Littleport labourers took
to organising themselves. So far no agreement had been reached
with the magistrates as at Brandon and Bury, and, having cowed
their own village, they began preparations for an armed march
on Ely the following day. There the magistrates could be forced
into making the concessions Henry Martin had suggested.

The incidents in Littleport until about eleven o'clock were
not directed by anyone of authority and had simply had revenge
as their objective, although the farmers were approached with
wage claims early on. At about this time, however, the crowd
sent for John Dennis, a licensed victualler, who was sympatheti-
cally disposed towards them. According to Mary How, his servant, Dennis was in bed when the crowd first called and she
said that they had to go back twice more before he would
agree to go. She also said that Christopher Butcher threatened
to shoot her master if he would not join the crowd, but Dennis
himself said that he got up and went to the market place because
he heard "beer was to be given". His defence at his trial was that
he was forced into joining the crowd, but his actions belie this.
It is reasonably certain that he took control of the preparations
for the march to Ely.

Dennis and the labourers reassembled at *The Globe Inn,*
where their plans for the following day (which incidentally was
Ely Fair day) were laid. It is more than likely that someone was
sent to Downham, a few miles away, to tell the inhabitants there
to make their way to Ely the next morning, and probably a
reckoning of who had and who had not been forced to part
with cash was made with a view to rectifying any oversights. Certainly Richard Burridge and Richard Nicholas went along in the
very early hours of Thursday morning and robbed Mary Morley,
Ann Cutlack, a farmer's wife, and Isaac Taylor, who was told
that "the mob which were then collected together at Littleport

were going to Ely to take the Town up to Government". It was
also decided to obtain arms, and Littleport was searched for
ammunition and firearms of any kind. John Green and Beamiss
went again to Wiles' shop (it is interesting to note that, until
Dennis appeared on the scene, the powder and shot were un-
touched) and took 7 lbs. of gunpowder and a barrel containing
56 lbs. of shot back to *The Globe,* where Francis Torrington
contributed another 5 lbs. of gunpowder he had taken from one
of the Cheesewrights. William Murfitt and John Warner
knocked up John Rust, a labourer who shot wildfowl, and
relieved him of two guns worth £10, while Burridge and Henry
Mainer, wearing handkerchiefs and scarves taken from Vachell,
took another, worth £5, from Elizabeth Stimson. Robert Salmon
took a gun from Cutlack and relieved Thomas Waddelow of
another. Somewhat later, an armed William Gotobed held up
Robert Whitworth (or Whitmore) and robbed him of a gun and
two pitchforks, saying he was off to join the crowd. Dennis was
seen by numerous people distributing shot at *The Globe* from
about one o'clock onwards, and Mary How said the labourers
had some target practice in the early hours. In all, the Treasury
Solicitors were told, seventy-three offences were committed in
Littleport during Wednesday and the early hours of Thursday,
23rd May.

Having armed themselves, the labourers looked around for a
means of transporting themselves and their firearms into Ely.
They went along to the farm belonging to Henry Tansley and
took a waggon and three horses from his stable. According to
George Stevens, the mob was ready to start the march at three
o'clock in the morning but the waggon had not then been got
ready. Eventually it was loaded up so that it looked like a primitive tank, and was driven by George Crow. "They had armed
themselves", a description said,

with the most dangerous and offensive weapons, such as Bludgeons,
Pitchforks, Muck Cromes, Fork Shafts headed with short iron
spikes, Fowling pieces and Fowler's guns, the tubes of which latter
are from 7 to 10 feet in length, carry about 2 lbs. of shot, and will
kill at a distance of 150 yards.

The procession, headed by the armed waggon and John
Walker, "carrying a pole in his Hand by way of a Signal", set
out for Ely during the early hours of Thursday morning. One
last piece of violence was committed in Littleport when Isaac

Harley and Thomas South caught sight of William Martin in the street. They demanded that the farmer should accompany them to Ely but he refused. Harley threatened to kill him and South knocked him down, but they left him behind. Another farmer, an old man named William Poole, was not so fortunate. He was working in a field near the turnpike road that led from Littleport to Ely when he saw an armed party on the road. In spite of protests that he could hardly walk, Burridge and Thomas Armiger forced him to join them. Quite a large number of others were similarly pressed into going.

The authorities had been warned of the approach of the crowd from Littleport, and a magistrate, the Rev. William Metcalfe,[9] met them on the outskirts of Ely, sometime between five and six o'clock. He asked the crowd to stop but Crow, driving the waggon, said, "Go on, go on, we will go into the market place."

A crowd, estimated by one observer at 500, collected in the market square outside *The White Hart Inn,* where a number of the magistrates (all clergymen) had gathered. Metcalfe and the Rev. Peploe Ward asked them what they wanted and received the usual replies. Richard Rutter added a demand for beer at 2d. a pint to the now familiar cry for flour at 2s. 6d. and an allowance or wage of 2s. The magistrates, who were by this time scared out of their wits, invited a deputation, led by John Lee, into the inn to discuss their claims and the following paper was eventually drawn up.

The Magistrates agree, and do order that the overseers—shall pay to each family Two Shillings per Head per week, when Flour is Half a Crown a Stone; such allowance be raised in proportion when the price of Flour is higher, and that the price of Labor shall be Two Shillings per day, whether Married or Single and that the Laborer shall be paid his full wages by the Farmer, who hires him.

During the deliberations in *The White Hart* the Rev. Henry Law,[10] another magistrate who had been asked by Ward to hurry to Ely, entered the room. He wrote a number of letters, now in the Cambridge University Library, justifying his part in the proceedings and they help determine what went on on that day. Law approved of the concessions. He told Sidmouth that increased relief from 1s. 6d. to 2s. "to the poor families receiving parochial relief was justified . . . My Lord, because the price of grain had become much higher (in May 1816) than when the foresaid allowance was made (November 1815)".[11]

The concessions were welcomed by the delegates, but they asked for one thing more—"forgiveness for what had passed". This was not acceptable to all the magistrates and an argument developed. Law told the Home Secretary that he warned the magistrates, as did Lieutenant Goodenough at Brandon, that they were acting *ultra vires*. "I resisted the compromise about to be made to the rioters," he wrote, "and I stated, that I would not agree to such terms which were contrary to law, reason and common sense, and I told the Mob, that he [Peploe Ward] had no power to hold out such a promise of pardon to them for that if they had offended against the Law, so their offences they must be accountable."[12] The delegates' reply to Law's prevaricating was *"then we have done nothing we will agree to nothing we will have Blood before Dinner"*. This was enough for the majority of the J.P.s and they agreed that "No person to be prosecuted for anything that has been done to the present time; provided that every Man immediately returns peaceably to his own Home". A statement of the magistrates' concessions was printed in an extraordinarily quick time and copies are still in existence. Vachell, writing to Law, said that he hoped that Sidmouth would be told of the way the magistrates were coerced. ". . . you know," he said, "that they were the absolute prisoners . . . at the mercy of a most ferocious armed rabble without any means of defence. Every allowance, I trust, will be made for their complying with terms, to which in fact they were compelled to agree."[13]

The result of the meeting with the magistrates was announced to the crowd who responded with great cheers and many, including those who had been forced along, returned to Littleport with the armed waggon.[14] Rayner Brassett, who had hidden and so avoided being taken to Ely, had followed the crowd there sometime afterwards with one of the Cutlack family and had returned to Littleport by nine o'clock. Shortly afterwards a group, including South, Jefferson and Little Easey, called on him and demanded food and beer. He accompanied them to *The Globe* and told Robert Johnson, the publican, to let the crowd have whatever beer they wanted. Brassett returned home but was soon called on by John Sparrow (who turned Crown witness) who said that more of the labourers had gathered at *The Crown* and that they, too, wanted food. The treasurer went along there and found Sparrow, Chevell, Beamiss and others drinking a barrel. Realising that the whole of Littleport was given over to carousing, he then called at *The George*, where John Lee and Burridge gave him more money, and at *The Turk's Head*, where he ordered another barrel—"the Mob", he told the magistrates, "said that all the Public Houses should be treated alike". He paid for what had been consumed so far out of his own pocket because, he said, Chevell knew what was in the handkerchief and he dare not touch it except in that firebrand's presence.

At noon Chevell and six or seven others called on Brassett. Adding two pounds more. Chevell counted out the hoard which amounted to £43 4s. 0d. He then turned to his colleagues and "proposed . . . that all the Publicans should fare alike and that the whole of the money should be spent on victuals and drink". They then departed and Brassett dutifully went his rounds settling with the landlords. At the end of the day a balance of £6 7s. 1d. remained which "was spent by the Mob in Victuals and Drink on the Friday morning". Brassett said that he acted his part simply through fear, a contention which rings true in his case.

Not all the labourers had returned to Littleport. While those that had were drinking, many of their colleagues were rioting in Ely.

After hearing of the magistrates' concessions, a section of the Littleport crowd—which had been joined by some of Ely's "refractory inhabitants"—began demanding beer from the local publicans. By about 8.30 they were joined by labourers from Downham and they made their way to the house of Henry Rickwood. "Rickwood," a prosecution brief said, "is a Miller, and resides at Ely and he seems to have been considered by the Rioters as peculiarly deserving of their marked attention." Henry Chapman summed up the general belief about millers when he said, "the corn is got into the great People's hands—Damn them—if they [we?] are all of one mind we will take it away from them".

Mr. Rickwood was not at home when John Dennis, who described himself as cashier, demanded "£50 as a douceur for saving [the] house and premises from destruction". Gotobed fired a gun into the place and Mrs. Rickwood sent her son, William, to see Robert Edwards, the Chief Constable of the Hundred of Ely and the agent for Mortlock's bank, to obtain the sum demanded.

William Rickwood saw Edwards and told him of the crowd's demands. The constable began walking back to the miller's house but en route met the labourers with Mrs. Rickwood. At first he refused to give them money and made the mistake of brandishing his constable's staff, whereupon he was set upon and beaten by James Cammell into changing his mind. He asked whom he was to pay the money to and Dennis—who had tried to restrain the crowd—said that he would "go in for Littleport"; Flanders Hopkin went in representing the Downham labourers, and Stephen Saunderson those from Ely. Edwards handed the three £16 each and had one shilling left. Asked who should have it, Dennis replied that it had to be "divided *equally*". Edwards placed the amount to Rickwood's debt.

A great number of women were in the crowd milling about the streets of Ely and Sarah Hobbes, a soldier's wife and the only woman actually tried at the Special Assizes, was particularly active. According to John Bacon, a constable, she led the crowd through the churchyard and away from Edwards' house saying "come along, come along . . . we will go to Cooper's, he is a bigger rogue than Rickwood".[15]

William Cooper kept a flour and grocery shop, and was regarded as a profiteer as bad as the unfortunate Willets elsewhere. The crowd of about 200 angry men and women began to call for "a crow or a mattock" to pull the shop down when Law and Metcalfe, the two magistrates, pushed their way forward. They managed to dissuade the mob from destroying the building but a cry of "five pounds, five pounds" was set up. The terrified Cooper handed over a note to Metcalfe who dutifully passed it on to Dennis. At this stage, the Ely labourers pushed William Atkin and Aaron Layton, a tenant of Cooper's and a master bricklayer, forward, saying that they wanted to be treated the same as the Littleport people. Cooper handed Layton, who later claimed he was acting under duress (a witness said he was "taken from the door of his Mother's by one of the Mob"), another note and the crowd gave him (Layton or Cooper?) "three huzzas and went away".

From Cooper's shop the crowd went to visit George Stevens, another miller. Dennis demanded £50, but, after haggling for some time, agreed to accept ten. For some reason, Dennis objected to Atkin, who was a carpenter "possessed of some property", acting on behalf of the Ely crowd, and the money was divided between him and Layton.

The rest of Thursday was given over to rioting and drinking in Ely, the publicans being forced to supply food and drink, as they had at Littleport. Most of the Downham and Littleport

people, however, left by the early afternoon, and, after this, the
authorities made some show of resistance. Some prisoners were
obviously taken for, at three o'clock in the afternoon, Aaron
Layton, Walton and Hunt were seen in Littleport asking for help
to get them released. This was refused, the locals saying that none
of their colleagues was missing and that the waggon had been
put away. Later on, Henry Chapman, described as a "yeoman"
on one of the briefs, also went to Littleport to ask for help. At
five o'clock he was back in Ely, saying this had been agreed
to and that "they had got four waggons loaded". This was an
exaggeration, but some armed men may have returned. Robert
Salmon certainly went and relieved Cutlack of the gun he had
returned during the afternoon, announcing that they were off
to release prisoners at Ely. Certainly, too, about a dozen *were*
released; this is confirmed by letters from Law and others.[16]

The Littleport labourers were well satisfied with their day's
work and the late arrivals joined in the festivities in the town.
Dennis, who had purchased ribands for the crowd, said
exultingly, "we have done everything well they give us credit
for it", and there were a few more incidents to record. Henry
Mainer went to the unfortunate Tansley, who ranked second
only to the Martins as an object of hate, and held him up with
a gun. James Wortley and Thomas Smith took a pound from
Matthew Waddelow. Apologetically, they told him that he had
been overlooked the previous night.

Downham had not been as quiet as Littleport, and there there
were some minor incidents perpetrated on their return from
Ely by a crowd led by Flanders Hopkin, John and William
Wilson, and Matthew, Thomas and Samuel Seakins. Alice Corn-
wall was robbed of 4s. and another inhabitant was threatened
but was left alone when he gave bread away. The Downham
crowd, however, were a spineless lot compared with that at Littleport. A description of an attack they made on the house of
Francis Tingey deserves quoting in full.

The prisoners[17] with many others assembled at the prosecutor's
House on the 23rd ult. and demanded Money—The prosecutor
having refused to obey the call an attack was immediately made
upon his window by the prisoners and their party—The prosecutor's
wife then took the Alarm and sent her son Francis Tingey with a
Flag of Truce to the Besiegers and he succeeded in saving the Citadel from further destruction by payment of a three shilling piece.

CHAPTER NINE

FRIDAY, 24TH MAY was the most eventful day in the story of the East Anglian riots. The Ely magistrates had sent for troops to Bury, and had deputised Law "to convey the intelligence" of what had been going on to the Home Secretary. He left for London shortly after the attack on Cooper's house. En route he called on the Royston Yeomanry Cavalry and a detachment of these was sent to Ely. Later, he went to see Lord Sidmouth and asked for regular troops to be sent to the troubled city.

Sidmouth did not seem to think that troops were needed but sent to ask an associate of his, Sir Henry Bate Dudley, to go back with Law and take charge of operations to pacify the troubled districts.[1] Dudley agreed and met Law the following day. They set out for Ely early on Friday morning.

Bate Dudley's name has already appeared in the narrative. He was the son of a parson and was born in 1745, the second son of twelve, oddly described as "come to his father in wedlock".[2] He took Holy Orders and entered his father's old living at Farmbridge, Essex, and later, while a curate at Hendon, was responsible for introducing Mrs. Siddons to David Garrick. He was also a patron of Gainsborough. In 1773 he gained his reputation as "The Fighting Parson", after taking part in an altercation involving a lady that made wonderful Press copy and came to be called "The Vauxhall Affray",[3] but this was by no means the last of Dudley's duels or scandals.[4] He became editor of *The Morning Post*, then started a number of newspapers including *The Morning Herald* and served a twelve month prison sentence for libelling the Duke of Richmond. He was a great friend of the Prince Regent's and brought the Church some unwelcome publicity when it was discovered that he squandered £28,000 on a living at Bradwell that eventually lapsed to the Crown after the Bishop of London had refused to install him on the grounds of simony. While in Essex, Dudley gained a well-deserved reputation as a progressive farmer[5] and a dedicated opponent of the poaching gangs.[6] In 1813 he became Rector of Willingham (Cambs.) and a prebendary of Ely in June 1815. His preaching was said to have been "of inferior quality"[7] and his biographer suggests that he would have been more at ease as a soldier than a clergyman. Cobbett, who loathed Bate Dudley, drew his readers' attention on the 8th June to what had been going on in East Anglia. The most active magistrates, he reported, were

Parsons, with the Rev. *Sir Henry Bate Dudley, Baronet,* at their head. Certainly a very *worthy* head. A more fit head could not have been chosen. I expect to see him Archbishop of Canterbury yet; or, at least, I should expect it, if the Right Reverend personage, who so worthily fills that chair were not so much younger than the Reverend Sir Bate.
     The truth is * * * * * * * * * *

Bate Dudley and Law arrived in Ely at 2.30 p.m., with another forty-two of the Royston Volunteer Cavalry under Captain Wortham, to find the place in an uproar. (Vachell and Peploe Ward had written to Sidmouth, asking for no less than "two full troops of Horse and a piece or two of artillery"[8] to add to the Royston Yeomanry and a seventeen-strong detachment of the 1st Regiment of the Royal Dragoons who were there under the command of Captain Methuen.) Methuen was at first held in check by the frightened magistrates in the same way that Lieutenant Goodenough had been at Brandon. The Dragoons paraded the streets but at about eleven o'clock an incident developed when John Hassett dashed from a crowd of twenty or more hostile labourers and assaulted Joseph Heamers, one of the soldiers. Grabbing the man's sword, Hassett was alleged to have said, "Damn your Eyes I have got your sword and will fight any of you you Bugger". Following this, fighting took place and Methuen's men arrested some labourers, including Wilson Wyebrow and some of his friends from Downham, but they somehow contrived to escape. This was the first stirring against the crowd for which Daubeny and Seymour, two J.P.s, were responsible. Bate Dudley, however, told Sidmouth that the mob had destroyed "dwellings, stacks and granaries" and blamed "My Brother Magistrates who had entered into an indiscreet amnesty with the Principal Insurgents".[9] His written accounts of the troubles were highly coloured and penned, of course, to glorify his own part. Nevertheless he did act with promptitude and considerable bravery—although he had the troops to back him up that the unfortunate Ward and Metcalfe earlier had not.
     Ely was brought quickly under control by the new arrivals

and Bate Dudley was told of the troubles elsewhere. "The continuing outrages at Littleport are so alarming," he wrote to Sidmouth almost immediately after he arrived in Ely, "that I am determined to dash at the insurgents without delay."[10] About ten more people were recruited from the populace and then Dudley and Law, at the head of "20 of the Royston Yeomanry, the Detachment of the 1st Royal Dragoons and some inhabitants of Ely, and part of the staff of the Cambridge Militia", went "full charge" to Littleport.[11]

A number of colourful stories gathered around the story of the attack on Littleport, none of which can be substantiated, but most of which are worth repeating. The Rev. E. Coneybeare, for instance, said that the rioters were hunted by a Hanoverian Regiment who combed the district "with true German thoroughness",[12] whereas in fact these troops had left the country long before May.

"Local tradition still hands down the tale of the poor thatcher," he recorded, "who was engaged on the roof of the great tithe barn at Ely (the largest in the kingdom) at the moment when a detachment of these foreigners was marching past. The usual thatcher's cry to his assistant, 'Bunch! bunch!' was interpreted by the German officer in command as an insult to his troops. On the instant he halted them beside the barn, and gave the order to fire. Pierced by a dozen musket balls, the unhappy thatcher rolled from the roof, his body falling upon the great folding door of the barn, which happened to be half open. There it hung, dripping with blood for over three days, the officer swearing that anyone who dared to remove it should share the same fate, as an example to all to behave with due respect to their oppressors."[13]

Another writer painted a fanciful yet dramatic picture of the events of Friday and a clash with Methuen's troops. The armed waggon certainly had *not* been taken to Ely again.

Next morning a report was circulated that the horse soldiers were coming. The waggon that was brought by the rioters on the previous day was placed at *The Lamb* corner, and upon it were placed heavy wash guns, charged heavily with slugs, and manned by pot valiant fenmen trained to command the road. Others with forks, cleavers, knives, and bludgeons had assembled, swearing they would cut down every soldier as he came up. About noon a cry was raised, "They are coming", and a troop of Dragoons from Bury came up the Gallery at a sharp trot, their carbines at hip, swords gleaming in the sunlight. The bright helmets, with the rattle and clank of horses' feet and military trappings were too awful for the warlike fenmen and their supporters; they bolted in wild confusion in all directions, some making off for Littleport, others creeping out of Ely the best way they could. Sir Bates [*sic*] Dudley was sent down also by Government to check further violence. Some of the principal rioters were soon overhauled, hoisted in a waggon, and thrashed through the streets. Dudley's ride, as it was called, spread terror throughout the fens, and a wholesale dread of incurring the wrath of Sir Dudley.[14]

While preparations for an attack on Littleport were being made, the labourers there were celebrating in the usual manner. Most of their time was spent in drinking with what money was left over from Thursday, and there were only a very few half-hearted incidents like those of Thursday. South went back to Josiah Dewey's and threatened him with a gun saying, "blast you, I have a good mind to shoot you in your House", and Cammell and Rutter led a crowd to the house of James Horsley, a thatcher, and demanded £5. Much of the spirit the labourers showed the previous day seemed to have gone, and they went away after Horsley had promised them that he would go along to Dennis's public house, a promise which he did not keep. James Luddington, a J.P., also argued with a crowd led by Joseph Irons, who went away from him empty-handed but threatening to return with "the foreman" (Dennis). William Walker was also threatened and told by Robert Langford that the mob was reassembling and that, unless he handed over money and gin, his house would be burnt down. It was generally believed that a plan was afoot to fire Littleport and Ely later during the day. Bate Dudley certainly thought so,[15] and William Crow was reported to have heard James Lee say that "If the overseers of the parish will not come forward this day (Friday) and pay all us [*sic*] two shillings per day for yesterday and today then woe be to Littleport tonight". Asked if he meant fire, he replied, "Yes", and told Crow to spread the news around. Long after the riots were over, reports appeared in the East Anglian newspapers saying an attempt to start something had actually been made in Ely.

"The design of the Littleport rioters to destroy the town of Ely by fire," it was reported, "has been manifested by a discovery, made within these few days, of a quantity of combustible materials, which were found in the warehouse of a Mr. Garratt, a respectable grocer of that place, secretly laid immediately under the floor where he kept his casks of gunpowder : amongst these combustibles was a piece of charcoal, the fire of which appeared to have been providentially extinguished from the want of air."[16]

When Bate Dudley and Law arrived at Littleport at about six o'clock in the evening, most of the labourers were in *The George*. Robert Stevens, a local surgeon, said that the Fighting Parson dismounted and commanded them to give themselves up. Cammell became abusive and Bate Dudley tried to grab him, but broke off the encounter when either Rutter or Daniel Wilson, the blacksmith, hit him over the head with an iron bar. The prosecution brief of "The King versus Daniel Wilson" in the Cambridgeshire Record Office describes this undignified treatment of the victor of so many duels thus :

N.B. The truth is that Sir H. B. Dudley attended by the Military went to the door of *The George* public house and commanded the Rioters to surrender upon which Cammell came out and stood in the Door way and said come on you Piccadilly Butchers (alluding probably to the military) upon which Sir Henry collared him and it was during the struggle between Sir H. B. Dudley & Cammell that this assault took place.

Shortly after the assault on Bate Dudley, shooting began. It is not clear who fired the first shots, but the labourers were no match for the military. John Simmons, one of the Dragoons, was knocked off his horse and a sergeant's knee was injured when he, too, was unhorsed. Thomas South seriously injured a soldier named Wallance, a Waterloo veteran, who eventually had an arm amputated and became a pensioner on the Littleport poor rates.[17] These were all the injuries among Bate Dudley's party, but among the labourers casualties were greater. Thomas Sindall was captured and then shot through the head by William Porter while trying to escape, and a colleague had part of his jaw taken away by a sabre cut. Isaac Harley was badly shot but lived to regret that "having three waistcoats on, prevented his death that day".[18]

Most reports of the incidents at Littleport said that two labourers were killed during the fighting, but Sindall was undoubtedly the only fatality.[19] Bate Dudley told Sidmouth there were two[20] and every journal and newspaper wrote in the same way, *The Morning Post*, for instance, saying so in the very issue that reported the Coroner's inquest on Sindall.[21] W. H. Barrett says that, according to tradition, two soldiers were also killed and not found until their bodies were dug up during excavations forty years later. It is inconceivable that their disappearance would have escaped comment at the time, however.[22]

The labourers scattered after the affray outside *The George*, chased by the soldiers. Fifty-six were taken into custody that evening and a further forty-two were brought in on the Saturday.[23] The chase was not without its drama and the Dragoons compared favourably with those at Norwich.

"We understand that after the firing ceased at Littleport," noted the *Norwich Mercury*, "two privates of the First Royal Dragoons, being in close pursuit of two daring offenders on one of the banks of the River Ouse, and the latter having taken to a boat and crossed the river, immediately gave their horses to a bystander and elevating their pistols with their left hands above the water, swam across the river with their right arms, to the opposite bank, and secured the two men, the river is of a great width."[24]

All over the weekend labourers were taken in and examined by the magistrates. The two Harleys and John Dennis, for instance, who had £25 in notes with him, were caught on the 25th at West Dereham. Many were sheltered by other labourers, one of whom was eventually fully committed to the Special Assizes for doing so. This was David Stimson who was visited by James Smith of Eriswell, Suffolk, constable,

who on his oath saith that on Saturday Evening the twenty-fifth day of May instant he went to the house of the Prisoner David Stimson who resides in Burnt Fen in the Parish of Mildenhall in the County of Suffolk for the purpose of searching the said house after some Rioters who were suspected to be concealed there that the said David Stimson told him this informant that he had, had half a Dozen secreted there the night before and that he would secrete them.

Some of the locals were zealous in their attempt to bring the labourers to book. One of the bills paid by the magistrates of Ely was for £1 3s. 5d. "Expenses for the apprehension and keeping in custody Thomas Tippell alias Gibbons on suspicion of being Jefferson a Littleport Rioter who was absconded".

Some of the labourers who ran from Ely, Downham and Littleport got well away, and Bow Street officers were employed to apprehend them. Aaron Layton was one who was caught in London. William Gotobed also got to the capital, but was never caught. He eventually returned to Littleport several years later after his wife and family had become chargeable to the parish and the locals had petitioned on his behalf. His brother, Thomas, had also not been caught by the time of the trial and Stephen Saunderson was another who went to London, got clean away and was never brought to book.[25]

The Bow Street officers were not very successful in obtaining their fees from the magistrates, despite the fact that they were reckoned to have been "of the greatest use, and were actively employed during the time charged by them". On occasion the Government would defray the expenses incurred in the hiring of an officer, and the Ely magistrates clearly expected they would in 1816,[26] basing their claims on the fact that the legal proceedings "were intended to have more than *local* significance". This cut little ice with the Treasury Solicitors and the Government eventually allowed £1,000 out of a total of £1,697 13s. 1d., the rest to be met locally. Lavender and Perry, the two investigators, wrote to Evans asking for their fees.

Bow Street Office
Augst 23 1816

Sir

When you was in town some time since you meet Mr Perry in Bow Street with whom you had some conversation respecting our Account when you was kind enough to say you would send us a Draft for the several allowance for our trouble and loss of time while in Ely including the residue of our Expenses.

I hope you will pardon the Liberty I have taken in thus Addressing you but being both of us much in want of Money at this time I hope and trust wil be a sufficiant Excuse

I am Sir
with the Greatest Respect
Your Obet Sert
L. Lavender.[27]

H. R. Evans Esq.

About eighty prisoners were eventually caught, sent before Bate Dudley and the other magistrates and fully committed for trial. It was decided to try them at Special Assizes, which, it was hoped, would attract great attention and serve as a warning to rioters in other parts of the country. According to Sidmouth it was successful in doing this.[28]

The Home Secretary also changed his mind about the need for sending more troops to the troubled areas. He had stopped the disembodying of the West Norfolk Militia on the 18th May[29] and promised to send troops to Brandon the following day.[30] Hearing that Ely Cathedral was in danger and that "reports from neighbouring villages" confirmed there was "a riotous disposition" prevailing, he despatched three troops of cavalry (100 men), two six pounders and three companies of the 69th Regiment there under the command of Major General Byng.[31] He also ordered the Lords Lieutenants to go to their respective counties, expressed grave dissatisfaction at the behaviour of the magistrates, and ordered the following proclamation to be displayed prominently in all the trouble spots.[32]

PROCLAMATION

Whitehall, 25 May 1816.

Whereas it has been humbly represented to His Royal Highness the Prince Regent, that a great Number of Persons, for some Time past, unlawfully assembled themselves together in divers Parts of the Counties of NORFOLK, SUFFOLK, HUNTINGDON-SHIRE and CAMBRIDGE, and have circulated Threatening Letters and Incendiary Handbills; held Nightly Meetings; and set fire to several Dwelling Houses, Barns, Outbuildings, and Stacks of Corn; and have destroyed Cattle, Corn, Threshing Machines, and Other Instruments of Husbandry :

His Royal Highness seeing the mischievous Consequences which must inevitably ensue, as well to the Peace of the Kingdom, as to the lives and Property of His Majesty's Subjects, from such illegal and dangerous Proceedings, if not speedily suppressed; and being firmly resolved to cause the Laws to be put in Execution for the Punishment of such as offend against them, is hereby pleased, in the Name and on the Behalf of His Majesty, to promise and declare, that any Person or Persons who shall discover and apprehend or cause to be discovered and apprehended, the Authors, Abbettors, or Perpetrators of any of the Felonies or Outrages above-mentioned, so that they or any of them may be duly convicted thereof, shall be entitled to the Sum of

ONE HUNDRED POUNDS

For each and every Person who shall be convicted of any of the aforesaid Felonies.

And His Royal Highness is further pleased, in the Name and on the Behalf of His Majesty, to promise His most gracious Pardon to any Person or Persons concerned in the violent and illegal Proceedings in question, upon making such Discovery as aforesaid, except any Person who shall have been a Principal in the Commission of any of the Felonious Offences above-mentioned.

The said Reward of One Hundred Pounds to be paid by the Lords Commissioners of His Majesty's Treasury.

SIDMOUTH

Johnson claimed that one person betrayed a rioter for the reward, but there were more than that, though none of them got any money. A letter in the Home Office papers says that there were seven claims in all, but goes on, "I have received Lord Sidmouth's directions to acquaint you that as None of the Persons for whose apprehension and conviction the Rewards are claimed, where found Guilty of any of the offences mentioned in the Proclamation of the 25th. of May, the Petitioners have no title to the rewards which they have applied for".[33]

Lord Suffield very quickly circularised the Commanding Officers of the Yeomanry Cavalry in Norfolk, saying that the "Corps under [their] command ... be kept in such a state of preparation that it may be assembled with as little delay as possible".[34] The Duke of Grafton met the Suffolk magistrates on the 27th May and issued a public notice. Rather late in the day, the authorities admitted the existence of distress and intimated that it might be possible to alleviate it. The magistrates' concessions, however, were criticised. It was decided

that the most patient and careful attention should be given, with a view of tracing the causes of these disorders, and of relieving, as far as circumstances will permit, the present distress of the Labouring Poor;—but that it is the decided opinion of this Meeting, that no concessions should be made, nor any Agreement entered into with bodies of people assembled in a riotous or threatening manner; and that the utmost exertions will be used to put down all tumults, and to bring to punishment all persons who may be concerned in such riotous proceeding.[35]

Sidmouth's decision to send troops to East Anglia and the magistrates' firmness—although belated—almost certainly prevented the riots spreading further. On the very day that the shooting took place in Littleport, there had been troubles elsewhere. There had been every indication that the affair there was but the beginning of a really widespread rebellion.

CHAPTER TEN

Between nine and ten o'clock on Friday, 24th May, a crowd of about twenty labourers from the village of Outwell marched the few miles to Upwell.[1] Bread (beer), and blood were again their aims, and incidents very similar to those at Brandon, Downham Market and Littleport took place. According to Robert Atkins, a constable, the crowd assembled at Outwell and was led by William Lister who was armed and who was heard to say, "Damn all constables and farmers." John Massey, who had gone to the village from Upwell, said to the crowd, "Come along and I'll fill your Belly with Beer and your Pockets with Money."

The crowd were met on the outskirts of Upwell by the Rector, the Reverend William Gale Townley. He remonstrated with them but was told by William Dawson that they were starving, and had no fears. "Here I am," Dawson told the Vicar, "between Earth and Sky—so help me God. I would sooner loose [sic] my life than go home as I am. Bread I want and Bread I will have." The crowd went on to the house of Daniel Dawson, a baker, who gave them bread "under Impressions of fear and to prevent Persons so tumultuously and riotously assembled from committing Depredations or Violence on his Premises". They then went to *The Duke's Head*, but the publican was in bed. John Lawrence, "Gentleman", argued with the crowd which, like that at Downham, showed little real spirit. Lawrence called Thomas Sheppard, a constable, to disarm Bowers of a bludgeon and three labourers were taken into custody and eventually lodged in Wisbech gaol. From a bill paid to an Ely constable for apprehending William Lister, which included expenses for a journey to Boston, it would appear that some got well away.

Dawson, Lister, Massey and Robert Lancaster were eventually committed to the Special Assize at Ely. They were among those set free on their own recognizances to keep the peace.

From Sidmouth's proclamation it will be seen that trouble had also spread into Huntingdonshire. At Ramsey a crowd, led

by John Brown, "lately...a private in the marines", had
attacked an unpopular overseer's house on the 19th and strip-
ped the tiles off his roof. William Barrett, who was drunk
and was well-known as being "fond of a little beer", and John
Bree acted as spokesmen. They demanded to know from Beard,
the overseer, "what wages were to be" and accused him of
attempting to lower them. They also went to a flour mill kept by
a Mrs. Gifford, "headed by a fife and horn", and, before breaking it up, told her they wanted lower prices next market day
and that the Whittlesea labourers would be joining them.
Barrett, Bree, and William Tibbs,[2] who was one of the few
labourers to speak in court on his own behalf, were eventually
tried at the Huntingdon Assizes. Chief Justice Vicary Gibbs told
them that, at one stage, he had considered dismissing them of
the misdemeanour charge they were on and substituting a capital
offence, but that the defence witnesses had changed his mind.
He sentenced all three to two years in the County gaol.[3]

The trouble in Ramsey continued for a few days and spread
to Warboys, a few miles away—although there are no Press
reports of violence there. The Huntingdon Volunteer Cavalry
went to both places on the Tuesday and things were reported
quiet by the following day.[4] This seems to have been the limit
of troubles in Huntingdon, as, a week or so later, a correspondent
to one of the local papers wrote complaining that it was unfair
of Sidmouth to have included the county in the Royal Proclamation. Troops, he said, had been sent to St. Ives, yet no trouble
had developed. All that had happened had been that the soldiers
had been entertained on the county rates—which were already
high enough.[5]

Essex had not been included in the Proclamation, although
there was more trouble there than in Huntingdon. At Great
Bardfield, on the 24th, a 200 strong mob, armed with axes and
spades, had collected to destroy mole ploughs and threshing
tackle[6] belonging to Philip Speir. The farmer and about twenty
others managed "by a Waterloo movement" to get between the
crowd and the barn to prevent any damage, but at Fressingfield
another crowd of 200 had assembled and destroyed machines
and ploughs both there and at Byton Hall.[7] An incident at Sible
Hedingham led to fighting with the military a few days later.

Threshing machines were smashed and the windows belonging
to the principal inhabitants broken at Sible Hedingham on the
28th May. Four prisoners were taken and lodged in the House

of Correction at Halstead, where, the following day, great numbers of armed labourers, including a large number of women, converged. The Halstead Yeomanry Cavalry were under arms and a magistrate read the Riot Act. Following this, the troops attacked the crowd who retreated into the churchyard. There they reassembled and counter-attacked, administering a severe defeat on their enemies. Since the Halstead Cavalry were unable to disperse the crowd, that night an appeal was sent for troops. A party of the 20th Dragoons arrived from Colchester the following day and the entrances to the town were guarded. Special constables were sworn in in large numbers, but the place was quiet from the 30th onwards.[8] There are no Press reports of anyone ever being prosecuted for these incidents in Essex. The troops left on 7th June.

In Cambridge and the Isle there were incidents other than those at Ely and Littleport. Soham and Isleham were centres which could have been trouble spots, and, according to one correspondent writing to the Ely solicitors, the people there were expecting the labourers from Littleport. He went on to say that, although they went to Ely, there had been some talk of them making for Soham, Mildenhall and Brandon. "If they had realised this plan," he concluded, "they would have shown some thousands in the field."[9]

At Wisbech, violence had been expected at the weekend of 25th May. The magistrates had written to Sidmouth on the 23rd, saying that the poor of the town had been unsettled since the riots at Downham Market and that inflammatory speeches were being made and placards had appeared threatening that the Downham Market labourers would be forcibly released from the town gaol on Saturday. On that day the place was packed with three corps of Yeomanry "in a very complete state of equipment" (120 men from Whittlesea, Upware and March), plus 300 special constables.[10] The prisoners were moved to Ely, regular troops stationed in the town, and violence was avoided.[11]

There was a panic in Cambridge itself at the time of the Littleport fighting which only subsided when the news of the labourers' defeat arrived. Great alarm was felt because of

the appearance of numerous knots of strange countrymen, coming in with large sticks, for two or three days past. Our Mayor, Colonel Mortlock, apprehending that this might have been preparatory to an intended entry of the Fen rioters, convened the Magistracy in the Town Hall this [24th] afternoon, who swore in three hundred of the principal inhabitants as special constables. *The Vice Chancellor, and Heads of Houses, also assembled, and resolved to put arms into the hands of the Students of their respective Colleges,* if found necessary.[12]

Suffolk, the scene of so many of the early riots, saw many more during this fateful period. At Stoke-by-Clare, James Mays was charged on the 22nd with threatening to set fire to stacks belonging to General John Tims Harvey Elwes, an extremely unpopular magistrate. Mays was discharged, but a crowd that had assembled outside the court broke up a threshing machine. Troops were sent to Stoke under a young officer named Frederick Coventry. They stayed there until about the 7th June and then left, despite the General's protests that he had had a report of someone saying "all was not over" and that nothing would be done while the troops were there.[13]

Grafton told Sidmouth on the 5th June that much of Suffolk had returned to normal. Violence had threatened when crowds of labourers turned up at the Monday meetings of the magistrates, but nowhere did they get out of hand. This might have been because troops had appeared and because what had happened at Littleport was well known. In the Hundreds of Napping and Mayland, crowds outside the House of Industry dispersed peacefully when appealed to, but in the Hundred of South Greenhoe conciliatory measures had to be offered to them. Feltwell was said to be disorderly, and in the Hundred of Shropham, where four labourers had been committed for breaking a threshing machine, a rescue was threatened but did not materialise.[14] At Metfield and St. James, a mob, led by an armed man on horseback, was alleged to have assembled on Greazy Green (?) on the 6th June, but no trouble developed, although they were said to have pressed people into joining them, and swearing oaths.[15] Grafton, despite saying that things were tranquil, asked Sidmouth whether the "specials" could be issued with swords, and the Home Secretary arranged for a number to be issued from Harwich to such persons as authorised by the Lord Lieutenant.[16]

By the middle of the first week of June, East Anglia was quiet, although it was an ominous quietness. Orders were given for the West Norfolk Militia to be disbanded[17] and the Special Assizes fixed to start on Monday, 17th June. The authorities felt, correctly, that, until it was over and examples made of the chief offenders, they were not free from trouble. Hugh Robert Evans wrote from Ely to Hobhouse, a Treasury Solicitor, on the 5th June.

I wish I could say that I am convinced that the danger is over. We are quiet, but it is the silence of sullenness—not of a subdued spirit, and I shall not be surprised if we have some Stacks and even Houses burnt. Murmurs and Whispers, and sulky Countenances, and invidious comparisons between Rich and Poor &c. &c. are among the symptoms of smothered Revenge. We are upon our guard and have a nightly patrole; but as the opening of the commission approaches our dangers and fears will increase.[18]

Major General Byng established his headquarters first at Newmarket, then Colchester,[19] and, despite the arguments of people like Elwes, contrived to keep his troops concentrated in groups as large as possible. The magistrates at Ely were obviously as frightened as Evans and wrote to Sidmouth that they expected trouble during the trials.[20]

Ely, June 8th. 1816.

My Lord
We the undersigned Magistrates of the Isle of Ely, being of opinion, that it would be dangerous to leave this place destitute of a military Force, request that your Lordship will be pleased to give directions, that the usual Practise of removing Troops during an Assize may be departed from at the ensuing Assizes here

We have the honor to be
My Lord
Your Lordships most
Obdt Humble Servants
W. Pearce Dean
Peploe Ward
George King
John Dampier
Wm Metcalfe
George Waddington

The Right Honble
Lord Sidmouth.

CHAPTER ELEVEN

PREPARATIONS FOR THE trials of the rioters were hurried on in Ely. Sidmouth would not allow a departure from the usual practice of denuding a town of troops during an Assize, despite an added appeal from Bishop Sparke who had expressed fears for the safety of the Cathedral,[1] but ordered Byng to show himself and keep his men nearby and in readiness for trouble.[2] The Town Hall was altered at a cost of £345 1s. 8d.[3] but Francis Bagge, the High Bailiff, expressed some doubts about the ceremonial arrangements. The trumpeters who "usually attend the Cambridge Assizes," he wrote, "are very indifferent ones."[4] Three judges were to try the offenders.

James Burrough (1750–1839), one of the judges chosen for the Special Assizes at Ely, had only been advanced to the Bench in May 1816, at the age of sixty-six, "a promotion he owed to the steady friendship of Lord Eldon". He had been called to the bar in 1773 and practised on the Western circuit. Following this, he was for a time deputy recorder of Salisbury and then recorder of Portsmouth. According to Foss, Burrough was noted for his great legal knowledge and kindness, his quaint way of illustrating his points and his aptness "to deal in apophthegms, one of which was 'Public policy is an unruly horse, which if a judge unwarily mounts, ten to one he is run away with' ". Burrough continued to sit in judgement in the Court of Common Pleas until 1829.[5]

One of Burrough's colleagues at the Ely Assizes was Charles Abbott (1762–1832), later the first Lord Tenterden. Born in Canterbury, Abbott was the son of a wigmaker who was said to have prided himself on his humble origins and whose epitaph, written by himself, was *humillimis sortis parentibus*. He graduated from Oxford in 1785 and was called to the bar in 1796. He joined the Oxford circuit where he had great success and took part in numerous state trials. His income was so large that he refused an offer of a seat on the Bench in 1808, but was finally elevated to a seat in the Common Pleas in January 1816. Very unwillingly, he was moved to the court of King's Bench

in May of the same year. According to Brougham, Abbott had
no striking forensic ability and Lord Campbell said that "he
never addressed a jury in his life".[6] Later in life Abbott succeeded
Ellenborough in the office of Chief Justice and established himself in the House of Lords as an opponent of reform. He sat in
judgement on a number of important state trials, including those
of Arthur Thistlewood and the Cato Street conspirators, Hone
and Cobbett. Abbott died in 1832 while taking part in the trial
of Charles Pinney, the Mayor of Bristol, for misconduct and
neglect of duty during riots in that city.[7]

If Abbott and Burrough brought solemnity to the proceedings
at Ely, the third member of the Bench added a touch of almost
Gilbertian farce. This was Edward Christian, the brother of
Fletcher Christian of the *Bounty*, and the Chief Justice of the
Isle of Ely.[8]

Christian had once been a member of the Northern circuit
but had gradually become little more than the subject of practical jokes played by his juniors, "who like himself had nothing
to do". He went back to the University of Cambridge and at the
time of the trial of the Ely and Littleport rioters was Professor
of the Laws of England. Christian is the subject of a cruel sketch
by Gunning who says that, on one occasion, when the authorities
of St. John's asked him to draw up a handbill warning unknown
characters who had pulled up College trees with legal proceedings, he threatened the culprits with "death under the black
act", a threat which produced the following epigram

> When Brunswick's great Duke, on a visit to France
> Led Austrians, and Prussians, and Hessians a dance,
> He thought to gain over the brave *sans culottes,*
> By kindly engaging *to cut all their throats* :
> So the Johnians, whose trees were most *cruelly mangled,*
> And *delicate sucklings* atrociously strangled,
> Invite the sly culprit who did the *black act,*
> To swing at the gallows, by owning the fact.

Christian was connected with a movement to promote a
savings bank in Cambridge "which it may be said involved many
persons in a heavy loss" and in 1805 took part in a disputed
election for the post of Registrar of the Bedford Level. Each
of the two contestants claimed a victory at the poll and Christian
barricaded himself for two days in the Fen office in the Temple
where the records were kept, but was eventually ousted. He

returned the following day in an effort to retake the citadel by a ruse but only succeeded in getting his head painfully wedged in the door until he admitted defeat and "*begged permission to withdraw it*". In his declining years, Gunning said, Christian was frequently seen in the public walks of Cambridge, "where his society was avoided by everyone whose time was of any value. He died in 1823, in the full vigour of his *incapacity*".[9]

Christian was made Chief Justice by the Bishop of Ely in 1800. Twice each year, according to Gunning, he "inflicted upon the Grand Jury of Ely a charge of unconscionable length", an unflattering description which is borne out by reports of his behaviour at the Special Assizes. Hobhouse wrote to Sidmouth that the Chief Justice's summing up was "unexceptional . . . except that it was too probing (?) and too pompous".[10] The letter went on

I hear that the language he uses to his confidants is that he has been most ill-used by the *Chancellor,* but I do not find that he has suggested in what way he would have had the Commission framed more respectably towards himself. For the sake of giving daily Proofs of his Absurdity, he refuses to come into Court in the Bishop's carriage with the others, and follows them alone in a vehicle of his own Purveyance.

Christian's bad temper is explained by the fact that there had obviously been a move to exclude him from the Judge's Bench. After the whole business was over, he complained to Sidmouth that "it certainly has been one of the greatest mortifications of my life, [that sixteen years after being made Chief Justice] my character was so little known to Your Lordship that you were led to think I was not a suitable person to act with His Majesty's Judges".[11] Perhaps Christian's character was *too* well-known to the Home Secretary! On the same day he wrote another letter to Sidmouth, complaining that the London newspapers hardly mentioned his part in the trial (this was perfectly true), "though it happened", he said, "that I had more points of Law to explain than the other judges together . . . It is a mean dishonest attempt to deprive me of my only perquisite viz the honour of my situation. For thank God I am now serving my country for nothing".[12] According to the entry on Christian in the *Dictionary of National Biography,* however, the Chief Justice received £1,500 a year. Whatever the facts were, he applied for loss of time payments, but with what success is unknown.[13]

The Press was not backward in urging the Judges to deal severely with the prisoners. *The Courier* contented itself with reminding its readers that "The result of similar disturbances [to those at Ely] a few years ago in Nottinghamshire was the execution at one time of about twenty unfortunate wretches".[14] This was typical. A theological journal in its monthly digest of news also advocated strong justice. "The event [the Royal Marriage]," it reported, "was followed by the distressing intelligence of dissatisfaction on the price of corn, which had broken into tumultuous riotings. These were chiefly confined to parts of Suffolk, Norfolk and Cambridgeshire. They who are at the head of affairs will follow Lord Bacon's advice we trust upon such subjects."[15]

On Monday, 17th June 1816, the proceedings at the Special Assizes began. A solemn procession led by the Bishop of Ely "with his sword of State borne before him (by his butler!)"[16] wound its way to the Cathedral and entered to the sound of Handel's air, "Why do the Heathen so furiously rage together", with the chorus of "Let us break their bonds asunder", sung by the choir. A special anthem was composed and sung for the occasion called "Tell it out among the people that the Lord is King" (96th Psalm, v. 10). Bate Dudley rammed the message home by preaching a sermon from I Timothy i. 9 "The Law is not made for a righteous man, but for the lawless and disobedient". "The discourse," reported *The Cambridge Chronicle*, "was delivered in a most animated and impressive manner."[17]

Abbott's address to the Grand Jury contained an explicit statement that the Government intended the business at Ely to be a warning to other would-be rioters. Poor seasons had aggravated distress, Abbott said, but the jury would have no great problems confronting them. "It is of the highest importance to the Peace and Safety, not only of this Isle," he went on, "but of the surrounding country, that all who read the account of its [the Assizes'] proceedings . . . may be convinced by the awful lesson which may here be taught . . ."

What Abbott meant by an awful lesson must have been very apparent to the labourers. The death penalty was possible for dozens of less serious crimes than those the prisoners at Ely were charged with, and all of them must have known of people who had received the supreme sentence. In the Assizes for Suffolk in 1816, for instance, death was pronounced seventeen times and one man executed, and in the Essex Assizes in the same year the totals had been twenty-nine and two.[18] Furthermore the poor, even if they could afford them, were not able to have counsel speak for them and had to make their final pleas themselves, an overwhelming task for an illiterate labourer. During the Special Assizes at Ely only a very few of those charged had anything to say in their own defence. A Mr. Hunt and a Mr. Hart appeared on behalf of a small number of them.

Abbott's charge to the Grand Jury was obviously prepared well in advance and was an integral part of the demonstration of force the Government was staging. Cobbett pointed out that, the very next day after the Judge had addressed the jurors, his speech was reported in full in the London morning papers. How did they get the report of it, he asked? Ely was sixty-seven miles from the capital and the copy could not have gone off before Monday evening. "What an able set of people follow these judges on this great occasion," he said. "There cannot be the smallest doubt, that the charge, &c * * *."[19] It is perhaps worth noting that it was three days before *The Times* reported the executions at Ely.

The trials lasted a whole week. Hobhouse had outlined the course matters would take, when he told Sidmouth on the 29th May that he would "endeavour to select the Cases, where the greatest outrages were committed, and the largest Number of Prisoners can be proved to have been engaged. I see no reason to doubt that the offences will be fixed by satisfactory Evidence on the Ringleaders".[20] Labourers were tried for thirteen offences committed at Ely and Littleport and many were found guilty. "All goes well," a report to the Home Office said on the 19th June, "our Judges are excellent: all around is tranquil, and it is evident that the Commission has produced the best effects."[21] The following day the same writer reported that Littleport was "panic stricken", awaiting the sentences which, he said, would "strike terror into the hard part of the inhabitants of this place".[22] Earlier in the week, the following resolutions had been taken by the churchwardens and overseers in the town, who envisaged the possibility of trouble when the fate of the labourers was made known.[23]

First That the Constables and Special Constables will attend to the instructions and directions of the Magistrates as to the regulations of the Parties standing idly in the streets of the Parish of Littleport. Third That the watchman shall be subject to the following regulations (viz) That Six Men shall watch every night four of whom shall be constantly on duty—To go out a half an hour after sunset and continue on Duty until an hour after daylight.

On the Friday the Judges announced that enough cases had been heard to set the populace an example and the labourers who had not already appeared were put to the bar. They were cautioned against the evils of drink and allowed to go free and told they would not be called to answer for their offences if they behaved. Each had to give a recognizance of £50 and find two sureties of £10 each.[24]

Henry Benson, the one farmer involved in the Ely and Littleport riots, and the subject of the fourteenth case at the Special Assizes, was bound over to appear at the next Assizes. He had ridden into Ely in the wake of the Littleport crowd and had been heard urging them to greater activity, saying he would "give them five hundred pounds to go on with it".[25] According to Samuel Andrews, a farmer who farmed near Benson in Burnt Fen, he had said at another time that he would give the labourers one hundred pounds to rise again. "My Men were there and durst not have gone unless I had given them leave when they went." Benson was charged only with a misdemeanour and the authorities had great difficulty in deciding what to do with him. His statements (his "confession" has already been quoted) are at variance with every other account of the happenings at Ely and Littleport[26] and it is perhaps best to regard him simply as an illiterate crank. There is a considerable amount of correspondence relating to Benson in the Cambridgeshire Record Office and it appears from evidence elsewhere that he was later given notice to quit his farm by the Earl of Hardwicke.[27] "It was never intended to proceed upon any of the indictments which were traversed[28] except Benson's which was reserved for further consideration," Hobhouse wrote to Hugh Robert Evans, when given a final decision on the farmer. "Since your letter of the 20th," he went on

I have brought the case under Review of the Attorney General and other Counsel; and it is thought advisable upon his complying with the Terms you suggest, not to proceed to his Trial. You are therefore authorised to assure him that Proceedings will be dropped upon his making a full Acknowledgement of his Error, and entering into a Recognizance to keep the Peace and be of good Behaviour for three years.[29]

On Saturday, 22nd May 1816, the sentences on those found

guilty were announced. Abbott lectured them, saying, incredible though it seems, that none were instigated by distress, apparently believing the contentions of Gurney, a prosecution lawyer, who had made much of the "great wages" they were alleged to have received.[30] Twenty-four were sentenced to death[31] but of these nineteen were reprieved.[32] Richard Rutter heard that he was to be transported for life instead; Easey, Jefferson, Chevell, Newell (who was one of the last to be apprehended and was still free on 8th June)[33] and Jessop were sentenced to fourteen years' transportation; John Easy, Mark Benton and John Walker were to be transported for seven years; and ten others were given twelve months in Ely gaol.[34] The five left to die were John Dennis and the elder Beamiss, who were told that their positions in life should have restrained them, Thomas South, Isaac Harley, who led the attack on Vachell's house, and George Crow.

After Abbott had pronounced sentence on the rioters, a thirteen-year-old boy, charged with a trifling offence unconnected with the riots, was brought before Christian. This gave the Chief Justice the opportunity to hold forth on the things uppermost in his mind. He alluded to the attempt to keep him off the Bench and repeated Abbott's contentions about most of the labourers being "robust men, in full health, strength and vigour . . . who were receiving great wages" and said that the sums of money that had been levied "were not intended to afford assistance to their families; but were to be spent in liquor, and thus to be applied as fresh fuel to the flames to their fury". The magistrates of the Isle of Ely asked for the Chief Justice's address to be printed and posted up throughout the countryside.[35]

Preparations for the executions were made during the week following the passing of the sentences. A military guard was put on the prisoners at Ely, and Bate Dudley was put in joint charge of security arrangements with Major General Byng.[36] A new drop was constructed, Evans reported, which, it was hoped, would launch "the unhappy men . . . into eternity without that horrible pause attending the usual mode of execution . . . from a cart".[37]

The executions took place on Friday, 28th June. The prisoners were taken out of their cells after "The Ordinary, the Reverend Mr. Griffith, had performed the last religious offices" and made to sit in a cart with elevated seats covered in black cloth. Johnson says that so great had been the sympathy shown for the condemned men that it had been difficult to hire a conveyance under five guineas, and quotes a receipt in the Muniments Room

of the Bishop's Palace at Ely which ends, "N.B. We have no
power of pressing a cart for the purpose, and 'tis a difficult
matter to get one, people feels so much upon the occasion". The
procession to the place of execution consisted of the magistrates
"with no less than three hundred of the most respected inhabitants of the Isle, on horseback, with white wands". All the
special constables and peace officers were in attendance, along
with three Chief Constables "their staffs of office covered with
black crepe".[38] The military once again were kept out of sight,
although there were rumours that a rescue by "the Bankmen"
was to be attempted.[39]

On the scaffold the prisoners addressed the crowd. There was
an altercation between them, when one admitted that it was
their intention to murder Henry Martin, although the Press
reports do not make the confession ring true. John Dennis made
a speech which was reported at length in the local newspapers.
"All you who are witness to this my disgraceful end," he said,

I exhort you in the name of God, that God before whom I shall
shortly appear, to avoid drunkeness, Sabbath-breaking, whoremon-
gery, bad company : oh! beware of these sins, I pray you also to
avoid rioting!—and in every respect refrain from breaking the laws
of your country!—Remember the words of the Judge, that tried us
for the crimes for which we are now going to suffer, who said, "The
law of the land will always be too strong for its assailants, and those
who defy the law will, in the end, be subdued by the law, and be
compelled to submit to its justice or its mercy!"—we stand here a
melancholy example of the power and justice of the law. I freely
forgive those who gave their evidence against me : and may the
God of mercy forgive me and have mercy upon my soul![40]

William Beamiss began to say, "I forgive Mr. Tansley that he
swore falsely against me", when the drop fell. "Dennis and he
were the most awakened; South was the most violent in his ges-
ticulations, but all were resigned."[41]

Local Press reports said that the bodies were delivered to relatives and friends, and buried the same evening (the bodies of
executed criminals could be interred in consecrated ground until
the 1830s). The Bury and Norwich Post (10th July) said that
there was a procession to St. Mary's Church, led by a company
of singers chanting the 104th Psalm and including the Chief
Constable and Benjamin Barlow, the keeper of the prison at Ely.
A correspondent of The Cambridge Gazette gave a different
version. Objecting to statements that the bodies had been handed

over, someone writing from Ely and signing himself "A CON-STANT READER", said the magistrates would not part with them. They were in fact

deposited in a room, at Ely, where the bodies lay a public spectacle to all who chose to repair thither to view them, until the evening of the following day, when they were buried in St. Mary's church yard, in Ely. It is true, the whole of the funeral service was read, both in the church and at the grave.[42]

Shortly after the executions, the following "voluntary confession" signed by the five dead men was made public.[43] It was said to have been drawn up in prison by a dissenting minister :[44]

We your poor unfortunate suffering fellow creatures, beg leave to present the public with this our last dying acknowledgement of the justice of that sentence, which has condemned us to die for the violent outrages we have committed, and hope it will be a warning to all, who may see, or hear of us, to avoid the like course. We acknowledge and confess our sins in general, and we most sincerely beg of God to pardon our sins : fervently hoping and trusting that God Almighty will, for the sake of the all-atoning merits of the Redeemer, receive our precious and immortal souls into his favour, though we have delayed their interests to this late hour; most earnestly entreating that the Almighty may grant us all our sufferings in this world, and none in the next. We most sincerely warn you all to avoid these sins, which have been the cause of bringing us here.

By all means avoid irreligion and vice of every kind, particularly that of swearing, drunkeness, Sabbath breaking, and that of shameful neglect of the means of grace, the only means through the merit of Christ, of our soul's salvation. We sincerely recommend to you, that you attend the public worship of God, particularly on the Lord's day, and most sincerely pray that all our friends and relatives will not put off their repentance to a deathbed, lest that God, whom they have neglected to serve while in health and strength, should say unto them at last, as he does to every neglector of salvation— "Because I have called, and ye refused; I have stretched out my hands and no man regarded; but ye have set at nought all my counsel, and would none of my reproof. I also will laugh at your calamity, and mock when your fear cometh.

JOHN DENNIS
W. BEAMISS

The marks of ⎰ THOMAS SOUTH   X
⎱ GEORGE CROW   X
   ISAAC HARLEY   X

In the presence   BENJ. BARLOW, Gaoler.

There were no petitions on behalf of Dennis and his friends, but trouble developed in Ely, when the prisoners who were sentenced to twelve months were taken away to the hulks. It was reported that Sidmouth had altered the sentences to seven years' transportation and the Press printed many letters complaining that the Home Secretary's action was illegal (or otherwise, depending upon whether the paper supported the Government or not). Jonathan Page, a farmer who employed 150 men, and a number of the inhabitants of Ely—some of whom had been prominent in the fight with the rioters—tried to hold a protest meeting in the Shire Hall, Ely, but were refused permission to do so. They were anxious to kill the impression that the inhabitants of the city were responsible for the increased sentences, and eventually held a meeting at *The Club Inn,* at which resolutions were passed, publicised and sent to the Regent, the Judges and the Home Secretary.[45] The whole business seems to have been a mistake, however, as there are reports of the prisoners returning to Ely from Sheerness on Monday, 2nd June 1817.[46] A letter from Abbott to Sidmouth blamed the Clerk of the Assizes for the misunderstanding. It was dated after Page's meeting had been held.[47]

Queen's Square
June 28 1816

My Lord
I have the honor to transmit herewith to your Lordship the memorial relating to the several prisoners who were capitally convicted and reprieved at Ely. Mr. Justice Burrough and myself are sorry the delay of the Clerk of Assize has prevented us from doing this sooner, and the more so, as we find our intended recommendations to His Majesty have been mentioned in the public newspapers, notwithstanding the cautions we gave to keep them secret until His Majesty's pleasure should be known.
I have the pleasure to remain

My Lord
Your Lordship's
Most Obd^t Sert
G. Abbott

Lord Viscount Sidmouth

The citizens at Page's meeting and the correspondents to the local newspapers also took the trouble to point out that Bate Dudley was getting practically all the credit for suppressing the riots, whereas Daubeny, Law and some other of the magistrates were (as has been pointed out) equally responsible. The Rev. William Metcalfe (who had by that time retired from the bench) was the subject of a vote of thanks.

The vote of thanks to Metcalfe, who had agreed to Page's Shire Hall meeting, was probably prompted by a similar vote of the magistrates to Sir Henry Bate Dudley. A public subscription to Dudley was opened which had reached the respectable figure of £179 13s. od. by the middle of June.[48] The fighting parson told Evans that he was delighted about "the measures so flatteringly recommended by the Earl of Hardwicke. If my opinion were asked of the resolution as affecting another instead of myself", he went on, "I should say they were exceedingly well drawn. Perhaps *The Morning Herald* not having the Advertisement [of the subscription]", he added, "might carry the appearance of false delicacy".[49]

Bate Dudley went on record as saying that he thought the authorities had made "a wise arrangement . . . about those to be transported and also those to be imprisoned",[50] but the news was greeted with horror throughout the area. Transportation to New South Wales had not been the practice for so many years.[51] What went on was, however, well known to the labourers and already there were pathetically named "Botany Bay farms" in existence.[52] Years later, Edward Gibbon Wakefield said that he knew of occasions on which two-thirds of the convicts embarked in England died en route to the settlement. This was because, he said, the contracts were made for so many taken on board and "not for so many disembarked in the colony; the consequence was that the captain of the transport had a direct interest in killing his prisoners, and the fact was that, as to a great number of ships, one-third; as to a considerable number, a half; as to some, two-thirds of the prisoners died on the passage".[53] *The Examiner*, early in 1816,[54] published a letter received from a convict sent to Botany Bay which makes dreadful reading. "I will state my usage on the voyage which was beyond belief," he wrote,

for we had the biggest rascal of a Captain that ever existed, but God rewarded him for it—he died and was thrown overboard for the sharks, for when we was in the hot climates, he kept us confined betwixt decks; we was obliged to strip us stark naked, and then the sweat ran down us like rain, which caused a brain fever, which went all thro' the ship; the men died like rotten sheep, but, as God would have it, I escaped the disorder, which was a miracle; for out of 200 men, only 20 escaped it; I suppose there was 150

at one time that could not help themselves to a drink of water, and
when we got near the harbour, there was only three that was able
to work at the ship. The Captain and the first and second Mates
was thrown overboard, and the third Mate was bedfast, and not a
man on board that could navigate the ship, and we made an unin-
habited part of the island; but at last we fell in with the Bloxebury,
that had women convicts on board, and we got assistance from that
ship, or else we certainly must have perished.

Chevell and most of his friends sailed for New South Wales
on the *Sir William Bensley* on the 9th October, 1816.[55] It is not
known what happened to them en voyage, or whether any of
them ever returned to the homes they were said to have dis-
graced.

It was the Government's intention to make an example of the
Ely and Littleport rioters and teach ill-disposed persons throughout the country to refrain from rioting. The harshness of the sentences (and of course the trials of the Downham, Norwich and
Brandon rioters were yet to come) and the display of force
seemed to have achieved these objects for a time locally. During
the trials, only a few minor incidents were reported and, after
the sentences were announced, even these came to an end. A
threshing machine was destroyed at Worlington, near Mildenhall,
a threatening notice displayed on a Mr. Booty's barn[56] and
incendiary letters were sent to the Rev. George Leapingwell of
Good Easter (Essex),[57] but that was all. East Anglia for several
months seemed stunned by the vengeance taken by the authorities.

The hopes that the example made of the fenland labourers
would deter others far away were not realised. The editorial in
the same issue of *The Courier* that printed the confession of those
executed at Ely commented that, whereas it was hoped that there
would be an end to disturbances, serious incidents had taken
place that very week at Loughborough and Frome, where a
detachment of Inniskillen Dragoons had had to be called to quell
the mob. These were but two of many trouble spots where the
lesson of Ely went unheeded.

It would be pleasant to be able to record that some alleviation
of the labourers' lot followed the rising of 1816, but poverty was
the cause of the riots, and poverty remained. A Select Committee was set up to look into the administration of the Poor Law

but it cannot be claimed that this was forced by the labourers' actions. As the year went on, prices rose even higher than they were in May and conditions became even worse for the rural poor. The introduction of machinery went on unchecked and towards the end of the year rioting began again in East Anglia. This time, however, it did not spread and was, in fact, similar to the early unconnected and often secretive incidents of April. As early as August, for instance, arson was reported from Tillingham (Essex); albeit that place is a long way from the centres of disaffection in May.[58] Two months later, however, a riot took place at Layer Bretton in which a threshing machine belonging to William Sachs was destroyed, an incident for which a half dozen labourers appeared at the Ipswich Quarter Sessions and received sentences of six months' and a year's imprisonment.[59] At Bury Quarter Sessions in October 1816, three labourers got moderate sentences for riotously assembling at Kersey,[60] and, at the following sessions, seven appeared for a riot and misdemeanour in Hitcham, one of the trouble spots in 1816.[61] Trouble also threatened near Diss,[62] and there was an incident at Duxford (Cambs.).[63]

Within a few years, riots of this kind were fairly common in East Anglia, and particularly in Norfolk,[64] but it is noticeable that places like Littleport and Downham Market remained quiet. Years later, the Whig Government, returned after the Reform Act, set about altering the system of poor relief. Questionnaires were sent out concerning the administration of the Poor Law. Question 53 was, "Can you give the Commissioners any information respecting the causes and consequences of the agrarian riots and burnings of 1830 and 1831 ?" Perhaps the answers from the trouble spots of 1816 are testimony to the efficacy of Lord Bacon's advice and the way it was acted upon.[65]

Littleport	"None."
Wisbech	"No burnings in this parish, but some very near us."
Ely	"We have not had any."
Holy Trinity	"No riots or burnings took place in this neighbourhood."
Upwell	"We had nothing of it with us."

NOTES

NOTES

CHAPTER ONE

1. *Passages in the Life of a Radical* (1844), pp. 6–7. R. F. Wearmouth, *Methodism and the Working Class Movements of England* (1937), deals with the troubles elsewhere in the country in Chap. 1, Part 1, "Luddism and other disturbances", p. 29 ff.

2. e.g. *A full and correct account of the Trials for Rioting at Ely and Littleport, in May, 1816* (1816); *Trials of the Prisoners at the Isle of Ely Special Assizes* (Cambridge 1816); *The Trials of the Rioters at Littleport and Ely with their Several Sentences* (Bury St. Edmunds, no date, presumably 1816).

3. e.g. The account in Vol. 1 of Harriet Martineau's *History of the Thirty Years' Peace* (this was reprinted almost word for word in many of the popular nineteenth-century histories of England, e.g. C. Knight, *A Popular History of England,* Vol. 8, pp. 59–60, and James Taylor, *The Age We Live In, A History of the XIX Century,* Vol. 1, p. 57); Spencer Walpole, *A History of England* (1913), Vol. 1, pp. 344–5; *The Riots in Cambs. (Littleport and Ely) 1815–16* "Reprinted from the earliest records, for R. A., a country gentleman" (Ely, 1890); C. Johnson, *An Account of the Ely and Littleport Riots in 1816* (Ely, 1893); E. Coneybeare, *History of Cambridgeshire* (1897), p. 257 ff; J. Wentworth Day, *A History of the Fens* (1954), Chap. 16; G. L. Archer, *Old Ely* (Ely, 1949). The accounts of the riots in the latter two books are almost entirely based on Johnson, as is that in *The Victoria County History of Cambridgeshire.*

4. E. P. Thompson, *The Making of the English Working Class* (1963), p. 67. Mr. Thompson discusses the controversial question of whether the labourers became poorer between 1790 and 1830 in Chaps. 7 and 10.

5. *Ibid.*, pp. 197–8. See also T. S. Ashton, *An Economic History of England in the 18th Century* (1955), p. 217 ff. and authorities cited there.

6. *Ibid.*, p. 220.

7. *Ibid.*, p. 67, and authorities quoted pp. 67–8.

8. E. Hobsbawm "The Machine Breakers", *Past and Present,* Vol. 1, 1952.

9. E. P. Thompson, *op cit.*, p. 63.

10. See p. 64.

11. G. E. Mingay, *English Landed Society in the Eighteenth Century* (1963), p. 11. See also Dorothy Marshall, *English People in the Eighteenth Century* (1956), pp. 195–7, and Ashton, *op. cit.*

12. TS/11/940/3381.

13. HO/42/150. See pp. 65–6.

14. J. H. Whiteley, *Wesley's England* (1954), p. 136.

15. E. P. Thompson, *op. cit.*, p. 197.

16. *Ibid.*, p. 177.

17. *Ibid.*, pp. 178, 197.

18. Most of the rioters caught for the incidents at Ely, Littleport and elsewhere signed their depositions with an X. The inadequacy of education in the rural areas at the time is well known, but might be illustrated by the following facts. In Norwich the Society for the Education of the Poor in the Principles of the Established Church was created in 1812, and seven years later there was a Bell system school catering for 200 children and a Lancastrian school with 250 boys. In Norfolk as a whole there were ninety-four schools with 4,600 children. *A Topographical and Historical Account of the City and County of Norwich* (1819). As late as 1846–7 "only 130 children, in a population of over 3,500 were being taught" in Littleport, "50 of them on Sundays only", *V.C.H. Cambs.*, Vol. 4, p. 102.

19. Quoted in E. P. Thompson, *op. cit.*, p. 92.

20. W. Hasbach, *A History of the English Agricultural Labourer* (1908).

21. *Ibid.*, p. 112.

22. T. Stone, *General View of the Agriculture of the County of Huntingdon*, p. 8.

23. R. Parkinson, *General View . . . of Huntingdon, 1811*, p. 87.

24. C. Vancouver, *General View . . . of Cambridgeshire, 1794.*

25. W. Gooch, *General View . . . of Cambridgeshire, 1813.*

26. N. Kent, *General View . . . of Norfolk, 1796.* See also W. Marshall, *The Rural Economy of Norfolk*, 2 vols., 1795.

27. A. Young, *General View . . . of Norfolk, 1804.* Chap. 6, *passim.*

28. Details of these Acts and awards were taken from the MS. of a comprehensive list covering the whole country shortly to be published by Mr. W. E. Tate.

29. Details of Suffolk enclosures are in W. E. Tate, *A Hand-*

list of Suffolk Enclosure Awards, in Proceedings of the Suffolk Institute of Archaeology, Vol. 25, Part 3 (1951). See also V. M. Lavrovsky, "Parliamentary Enclosures in the County of Suffolk (1797–1814)", *Economic History Review,* Vol. 7, No. 2, May 1937.

30. Lord Ernle, *English Farming Past and Present* (1961, 6th edit.), p. 249 ff. J. L. and B. Hammond, *The Village Labourer* (1911). W. H. R. Curtler, *The Enclosure and Redistribution of Our Land* (Oxford, 1920). A. H. Johnson, *The Disappearance of the Small Landowner* (Oxford, 1909). See also W. E. Tate, "Opposition to Parliamentary Enclosure in Eighteenth Century England", *Agricultural History,* July 1945, pp. 137–42.

31. W. H. R. Curtler, *op. cit.,* p. 164 ff. There are disputes about the actual extent to which enclosure contributed to the decline of the small owner, however. See e.g. E. Davies, "The Small Landowner, 1780–1832 in the Light of the Land Tax Assessments", *Economic History Review,* Vol. 1, Jan. 1927.

32. Lord Ernle, *op. cit.,* p. 299.

33. *Inquiry into the Propriety of Applying Wastes to the Better Maintenance and Support of the Poor* (1801). See also Paul Mantoux, *Industrial Revolution in the Eighteenth Century* (1961 ed.) and the quotations taken from official sources on p. 179, f.n. 5.

34. J. D. Chambers, "Enclosure and Labour Supply in the Industrial Revolution", *Economic History Review,* 2nd series, Vol. 5, 1952–3, p. 326. D. Marshall, *op. cit.,* p. 245.

35. A. Young, *General View . . . of Essex,* Vol. 1, p. 179.

36. W. Gooch, *op. cit.,* p. 82.

37. *Ibid.,* p. 84.

38. *The Cambridge Chronicle,* 16th June 1815. The rest of the scale included £15 15s. 0d. "for a conviction for burglary, £5 5s. 0d. for stealing a bullock, cow or beast or any threshed corn." See also the *Norwich Mercury,* 8th April 1815, for a public announcement regarding the "Association for Prosecuting Horse Stealers & Other Felons, *within* the Hundreds of Freebridge, Lynn, Marshland and Smithdon in the County of Norfolk". There is an article on the Eye Association by Mr. Eric Pursehouse in *The Diss Express,* 14th June 1963.

39. The Lopham Enclosure Act was passed in 1812.

40. *The Cambridge Chronicle,* 7th April 1815.

41. *Norwich Mercury,* 1st April 1815.

42. Treasury Solicitor's Papers TS/11/1041/4468. Prosecu-

tion brief of King v. Cracknell and others, John Thorp's evidence, see p. 87.

43. *General View . . . of Suffolk*, p. 204.

44. R. Parkinson, *op. cit.*, p. 270.

45. Lord Ernle, *op. cit.*, pp. 312, 315. For a discussion of the level of agricultural wages for the country as a whole see Sir J. Clapham, *An Economic History of Modern Britain,* "The Early Railway Age" (Cambridge, 1926) and the sources quoted there, and E. P. Thompson, *op. cit.*, Chap. 7.

46. p. 56.

47. A. Young, *General View . . . of Norfolk*, p. 493.

48. Chap. 13, p. 376.

49. Chap. 14, p. 285 ff.

50. W. Marshall, *op. cit.*, Vol. 1 p. 41.

51. p. 379.

52. ". . . on an arable farm in the pre-machine era, hand-threshing could form one-quarter of the total year's work." N. Gash, "Rural Unemployment, 1815–34", *Economic History Review*, Vol. 6, No. 1, October 1935, pp. 92–3.

53. T. Stone, *General View . . . of Huntingdon* (1793). E. P. Thompson, *op. cit.*, deals at considerable length in Chaps. 7 and 8 with the question of "average" wages and wholesale, and usually ignored, unemployment. "If there comes a frost they [the farmers] discharge them [the labourers]," said one overseer : "when the season opens they come to me, and take 'em back again." . . . "Wet weather created a 'surplus' : harvest a 'shortage'." *Ibid.*, p. 224. See also A. Redford, *Labour Migration in England* (2nd edit., 1963), p. 90. There is a considerable literature setting out to prove that employment increased after enclosure. Even if that were so, however, the fact remains that nowhere in East Anglia in 1816 were there enough jobs for the labourers. For a contemporary view on this question see C. D. Bereton, *A Practical Inquiry into the Number, Means of Employment and Wages of Agricultural Labourers* (Norwich, no date). Also J. D. Chambers, *op. cit.*

54. *General View . . . of Norfolk,* p. 484. See also E. W. Bovill, *English Country Life 1780–1830* (1962), Chap. 3, p. 31 ff. D. Marshall, *op. cit.*, p. 239.

55. J. Clapham, "The Early Railway Age", *op. cit.*, p. 122. See also p. 453. A. Redford, *op. cit.*, p. 77.

56. Quoted in W. Smart, "Antecedents of the Corn Law of 1815", *English Historical Review*, Vol. 24, 1909. Cobbett also

continually complained about the fine manners and gracious living affected by the farmers in these years. The following extract from *The Cambridge Gazette* suggests that some of them found the old ways still satisfactory. A farmer at Saffron Walden while eating with his friends went to carve "for his own use, the wing of a fowl, [and] very unluckily helped himself to a gentleman's middle finger. This accident was occasioned", the report concluded, "by the eagerness of the company who all had their hands in the dish at the same time". 6th April 1816.

57. E. Halévy, *A History of the English People in 1815* (Penguin edit.), Vol. 2, p. 63.

58. W. Gooch, *op. cit.*, p. 31.

59. *Ibid.*, p. 293.

60. A. Young, *General View . . . of Suffolk* (1797), p. 11. On rural housing see also Sir J. Clapham, "The Early Railway Age", p. 27 ff., *op. cit.* J. Howitt, *Rural Life of England* (1838), Vol. 2, Part 3, Chap. 1, and G. E. Fussell and C. Goodman, "Housing of the Rural Population in the Eighteenth Century", *Economic History*, supplement to the *Economic Journal*, Vol. 2, No. 5, Jan. 1930.

61. *The Village,* Book 1. Crabbe (1754–1832) was a native of Aldeburgh, Suffolk, and so is particularly reliable as a commentator on conditions in East Anglia. He went to schools at Bungay and Stowmarket and then worked in Wickhambrook. Edmund Burke got him a position in the Church of England and he was for a time curate at Aldeburgh.

62. "In psychological terms, this felt very much like a decline in standards. His own share in the 'benefits of economic progress' consisted of more potatoes, a few articles of cotton clothing for his family, soap and candles, some tea and sugar, and a great many articles in the *Economic History Review*." E. P. Thompson, *op. cit.*, p. 318.

63. *Victoria County History of Cambs.*, Vol. 2, p. 81. One farm by the Hundred Foot River of 293 acres fluctuated in value, as a result of the floods, from £800 to £1,200 in the eighteenth century. Owing to the serious inundations in the 1760s it then declined in value to £200. In 1805, when new drainage measures had been taken, the owner said he would not take £1,500 for it, *Ibid.*, Vol. 4, article on Downham, p. 90.

64. W. Gooch, *op. cit.*, p. 5. See also S. H. Miller and S. B. J. Skertchly, *The Fenland Past and Present* (1878), Chap. 13, "Sanitary Condition of the Fens".

CHAPTER TWO

1. R. Parkinson, *op. cit.*, p. 282. On the decline in the domestic industry of lace making in Hunts., see the evidence of the Rev. Hugh Wade Gery in the *Report from the Lords Committees on the Poor Laws, 1818.*

2. Grafton to Sidmouth, 29th April 1816, HO/42/149. At Bury itself, which "Not being a town of trade" and where "the principal employment of the lower classes is making worsted yarn", things were equally as desperate. Papers relating to Suffolk. (B.M. Ref. 1035 i 10.)

3. Sir J. Clapham, "The Transference of the Worsted Industry from Norfolk to the West Riding", *Economic Journal*, Vol. 20, 1910.

4. See A. Young, *General View . . . of Suffolk,* for an estimate of the number of spinners and combers in Suffolk in 1797, for instance, p. 209, ff.

5. *General View . . . of Essex, op. cit.*, p. 393.

6. *Ibid.* See also Thomas Cromwell, *The History of Colchester* (Colchester, 1825), where "the entire decay of the *Bay and Say Trade*" is put down to "the gradual advancement of the agricultural interest . . . to its recent climax of wealth and refinement, having created a demand for the productions of the general shop-trade"; p. 165.

7. J. Evans and J. Britton, *The Beauties of England*, Vol. 11, Norfolk (1810), p. 146. See also F. Eden, *The State of the Poor* (abridged edit., edited by A. G. L. Rogers, 1928), on Norwich. He said the decline was also due, as it certainly was in part, to the popularity of cotton, and he traced the decline in a weaver's wages from £1 1s. od. to 7s. to 8s. a week. See also Clapham, *Economic Journal, op. cit.*, and "The Decline of Norwich", M. F. Lloyd Pritchard, *Economic History Review*, 2nd series, Vol. 3, No. 3, 1951.

8. *Report from the Select Committee on the Poor Laws 1817,* p. 125. "Halstead had, twenty years ago, a flourishing woollen manufactory of says and baize; that manufactory about the year 1800 almost entirely ceased." *Ibid.* Evidence of John Vaizey.

9. *Ibid.* William Rankin's evidence, p. 158.

10. F. Schoberl, *The Beauties of England*, Vol. 14, Suffolk, pp. 152, 158, 213.

11. Lord Ernle, *op. cit.*, p. 312. Hemp passed through the hands of the grower, breaker, heckler, spinner, whitester, weaver and bleacher. When Young wrote the Suffolk report in 1797 the hemp weavers there were earning 16s. to 18s. a week. The remark above about workers connected with the hemp trade applying for relief is based on an examination of the parish records of Diss, Dickleburgh, Denton and Needham (all in Norfolk). Copies of these were very kindly loaned to me by Mr. E. Pursehouse of Diss. There are, of course, equally as many applicants for relief from the wool and linen trades.

12. C. Vancouver, *General View . . . of Cambridge.*

13. *General View . . . of Norfolk.* Young gives a good description of the incredibly complicated business of harvesting hemp in his *General View . . . of Cambridge.* Apparently little was grown in Huntingdon. One of the merits of hemp growing was that it needed no weeding as it destroyed every other plant. Young wrote of one piece of land at Hoxne where the crop had been grown continually for seventy years. See also *Annals of Agriculture,* Vol. 10, p. 377, on the cultivation of hemp in Suffolk. The growing and cultivation of flax also declined at the same time as that of hemp.

14. A. Young, *General View . . . of Suffolk*, p. 122. The hemp was often woven into fine cloth for shirts, table linen, etc., but was more often used in sacking and rope making, for instance, at Diss. *Suffolk Gentleman's Year Book* (Ipswich, 1815). The making of straw plat fabric at places like Coggeshall, Braintree, Bockingham, etc., was another minor source of work for some of the population of Eastern England.

15. J. L. and B. Hammond, *op. cit.*, p. 112 ff. For the Settlement Laws see also Hasbach, *op. cit.*, Chap. 3. C. R. Fay, *Life and Labour in the Nineteenth Century* (1933), Chap. 4. A. Redford, *op. cit.*, Chap. 5 and S. and B. Webb, *English Poor Law History* (1927), Vol. 1, Chap. 5.

16. A. Redford, *op. cit.*, p. 95–6.

17. A special case heard at the Court of Quarter Sessions at Kirton, Lincs., determined in May 1816 that a married man "hired by the year as a confined servant in husbandry" and living in a tied cottage did not qualify for a settlement. "In the hands of the servant, the house is connected with the service, and necessary for the performance of it, and cannot be considered

such a tenement as confers a settlement." *The British Volunteer*, 13th July 1816.

18. Evidence of John Bennett, a parish officer, p. 133. During the labourers' revolt of 1830 Bennett, then an M.P., was a particular object of hatred and was attacked in his parish of Hindon. J. L. and B. Hammond, *op. cit.*, p. 261.

19. J. Evans and J. Britton, *op. cit.*, p. 109.

20. *Victoria County History of Cambridgeshire*, Vol. 2, p. 96. S. and B. Webb, *op. cit.*, p. 347, f.n. 2, for Henry Crabbe Robinson's description of the ridiculous lengths to which litigation under the Settlement Laws could and often did go. Fielding has a description of how the Settlement Laws could be used to get rid of villagers in *Joseph Andrews*.

21. *Report from the Select Committee on the Poor Laws 1817*, p. 160.

22. 12th January 1816.

23. Chap. 6

24. The labourers resisted this. See the Hammonds and the replies to a questionnaire sent out by Arthur Young including "Has any article of food, as a substitute to wheaten bread, been successfully used?" *Annals of Agriculture,* Vol. 24.

25. *The Courier*, 10th September 1816.

26. *Ibid.* Another organisation of the same type was the Association for the Relief of the Labouring Classes. Created in 1812 it had raised £35,000 by 1816. See the address it issued that year in e.g. *The Christian Observer*, August 1816.

27. S. and B. Webb, *op. cit.*, pp. 131, 134.

28. *Ibid.*, p. 129. On the Poor Law in Cambridgeshire where the situation was different see E. Hampson, *Treatment of Poverty in Cambridgeshire* (1934). From about the 1730s "about one-tenth of the villages in Cambridgeshire" formed "some kind of an institution—far more often a poor house than a disciplinary industrial establishment". The workhouse was often farmed out in Cambridgeshire—and particularly in the Isle of Ely.

29. M. D. George, *England in Transition* (Pelican, 1962), p. 98. S. and B. Webb, *op. cit.*, p. 141. A. Young, *General View . . . of Suffolk*, p. 246. R. Wearmouth, *Methodism and the Common People of the Eighteenth Century* (1945), p. 83. J. J. Raven, *History of Suffolk* (1895), p. 271. J. L. and B. Hammond, *op. cit.*

30. F. Eden, *op. cit.*, p. 248.

31. A. Young, *General View . . . of Suffolk*, p. 216.

32. F. Eden, *op. cit.*, p. 253. The two large workhouses in

Norwich were interesting, one being "formerly a palace of the Duke of Norfolk, and the other a monastery".

33. "Speech of J. C. Curwen in the House of Commons on 28th May 1816 on a motion for a committee for considering the state of the Poor Laws". *The Pamphleteer*, Vol. 8, 1816.

34. *Extracts from the Information received by Her Majesty's Commissioners as to the Administration and Operation of the Poor Laws* (1837), p. 131 ff.

35. F. Eden, *op. cit.*, p. 314. S. and B. Webb, *op. cit.*, p. 160. "In one of the bye-laws of a neighbouring hundred house," wrote the Rector of Little Massingham, Norfolk, "one of the badges authorized by law is not the S to signify slave, nor the V to signify vagrant, nor the large Roman P to signify pauper, but it is to be written out in full length thus 'Infamous Liar'." C. D. Bereton, *An Inquiry into the Workhouse System and the Law of Maintenance in Agricultural Districts* (Norwich, no date, possibly 1825).

36. *The Village*. Young described the overcrowding in the Nacton house of industry in the *General View . . . of Suffolk*. "In the dormitory for men and boys, two men are usually put into a bed, and three or four boys, certainly too many; one man, or two boys, is the proper number; probably it arose from this circumstance, that the dormitory was neither neat nor sweet; dining hall very neat."

37. *General View . . . of Suffolk*, p. 246.

38. *Victoria County History of Cambridgeshire*, Vol. 2. A general scale for the whole country was not adopted, however, until 1821. Out-door relief had, of course, always been an accepted part of poor law practice whether given by the parish or an incorporation. Gilbert's Act of 1782 "which had as its main object the establishment by unions of parishes of reformed workhouses" specifically ordered the provision of "some weekly or other relief" in certain circumstances. S. and B. Webb, *op. cit.*, pp. 170–1. For the mercantilist conceptions regarding the necessity for low wage rates that are a background to Speenhamland see D. Marshall, *op. cit.*, p. 248.

39. *General View . . . of Suffolk*, p. 247.

40. "Observation on the State of Pauperism", *The Pamphleteer*, Vol. 10, 1817, No. 20.

41. "Thoughts on the Present Crisis", W. Peter, Vol. 8, 1816, No. 15.

42. *Ibid.*, p. 3.

43. *Ibid.,* p. 5.

44. *Ibid.*

45. *Ibid.*

46. In Papers relating to Suffolk (B.M. Ref. 10351 i 10).

47. *Extracts from the Information received by Her Majesty's Commissioners as to the Administration and Operation of the Poor Laws* (1837), p. 148.

48. N. Gash, *op. cit.,* p. 93. A. Redford, *op. cit.,* pp. 81–2.

49. *The Agricultural State of the Kingdom* (1816), Reply of Mr. Edward Moor, p. 312.

50. Hasbach, *op. cit.,* p. 208 and f.n. 2.

51. Chap. 12, in Bovill, *op. cit.,* is an extremely good account of the developments of these years, although it does not mention the associations.

52. Orridge, who was paid £300 per year, gave some interesting evidence about the state of prisons near this period which probably explains in part why so much resistance was put up by the poachers. He was a great believer in the merits of the treadmill and described one recently installed at Bury with gusto. It employed eighty-four men who spent twelve hours a day on it, with two hours off for meals. They walked, he calculated, "48–50 steps in a minute, and each step 7 inches apart". *Report from the Select Committee on Criminal Commitments and Convictions 1827,* p. 44. There is a survey of prisons in Suffolk in *Cuttings from Newspapers, etc., Relating to Suffolk 1806–17.* (B.M. Ref. 1035 i 9.)

53. *Report from the Select Committee on Criminal Commitments and Convictions 1827,* p. 39.

54. Other means of fighting the poachers, apart from the appointing of increasing numbers of keepers were the setting of traps, spring guns and other devices.

55. "The St. Neots Association for the Preservation of Game and Fish, and Prosecuting Poachers &c." had among its members the Duke of Manchester, the Earl of Sandwich, the Lord Bishop of Lincoln, Sir M. Burgoyne, Bart., General Onslow, the Right Honourable Lord Ongley, *et al.* It drew up a scale of rewards which were printed in the local newspapers. They were as follows :

Rewards	£	s.	d.
Unqualified persons, shooting, coursing or otherwise destroying game	5	0	0

Snarers, and night setters of game	10	0	0
Buying or selling any hare, pheasant, partridge, or other game	5	0	0
Taking or destroying fish in any river, pond, or water, belonging to any member of this association	5	0	0
Tracing or coursing in the snow	3	3	0
Killing a leveret in harvest or at any other time ...	2	0	0
Unqualified persons, keeping or using nets or other engines for taking fish	1	0	0

And for every other offence, such reward as a committee of any three of the members shall think fit.

56. *Report from the Select Committee on Criminal Commitments and Convictions 1827, op. cit.*, p. 21, also *The Report from the Committee on the Nature and Effect of the Game Laws* (1816), p. 3.

CHAPTER THREE

1. Halévy, *The Liberal Awakening* (1923), *passim* for the events of 1815–16. On the condition of agriculture at the end of the war see also Lord Ernle, *op. cit.*, Chap. 15, also G. E. Fussell and M. Compton, "Agricultural Adjustments after the Napoleonic Wars", *Economic History* supplement of *The Economic Journal*, Vol. 3, No. 14, February 1939.

2. *Age of Bronze.*

3. For the way wages were being reduced in East Anglia see e.g. *The Report from the Select Committee on Petitions Relating to the Corn Laws*, the evidence of James Buxton of Essex, and John Bennett, p. 55, ff.

4. Cambridgeshire Record Office. Papers relating to the Ely and Littleport riots, uncatalogued. Cited hereafter as C.R.O.

5. *The Agricultural State of the Kingdom in February, March and April 1816: being the Substance of the Replies of many of the most Opulent and Intelligent Landowners to a Circular Letter sent by the Board of Agriculture, to every part of England, Wales and Scotland.* (1816.) The Government tried to stop publication of this volume and it was always referred to as the "suppressed volume of the Board of Agriculture". It was extensively reviewed and made a great impression at the time. In all the reviews consulted, however, little real concern was shown at the facts elicited by question 8 quoted above. For

typical reviews see e.g. *The Norfolk Chronicle*, 14th Sept. 1816, *Bury Post*, 23rd Oct. 1816, *The British Review* 1816, Art. 21, p. 441 ff, *The London Chronicle,* 7th May 1816.

6. *Ibid.*, p. 41.

7. *Ibid.*, p. 303.

8. *Ibid.*, p. 310.

9. *Ibid.* Evidence of the Rev. James Buck, p. 324.

10. *Ibid.* Evidence of the Rev. St. John Priest, p. 191.

11. *Ibid.*, p. 192.

12. *Ibid.*, p. 195.

13. *Ibid.* Evidence of Samuel Taylor, junior. In any number of Government reports there are tables of expenditure in Poor Law areas, all of which show a great increase in 1816. The table for the expenditure under the heading "Unemployed" in Blything Hundred was given in the *Report from the Select Committee on Labourers Wages*, and reprinted in Hasbach, *op. cit.*, p. 183. It shows an increase from £5 18s. 6d. in 1815 to £1,384 3s. 3d. the following year.

14. Average prices of corn in England and Wales. By quarter of eight Winchester Bushels.

	Wheat	Rye	Barley	Oats
February	52s. 6d.	33s. 2d.	24s. 8d.	18s. 7d.
March	56s. 6d.	33s. 4d.	24s. 8d.	18s. 5d.
April	54s. 8d.	32s. 6d.	23s. 6d.	17s. 8d.
May	59s. 1d.	33s. 9d.	24s. 3d.	18s. 9d.
June	76s. 4d.	40s. 5d.	28s. 9d.	21s. 7d.

from *The New Monthly Magazine*, Vol. 5, 1816.

15. *Agricultural State of the Kingdom*, p. 320.

16. *Ibid.*, p. 301.

17. *The Cambridge Chronicle* of 2nd February 1816 contains three accounts of poaching violence, in one of which one of the offenders was mortally wounded.

18. *The Cambridge Gazette*, 3rd February 1816.

19. See later p. 90.

20. See the anonymous letter on p. 65–6 which shows the labourers regarded these campaigns as selfish and as models to be followed.

21. In 1814 the farmers had asked for limits of 84s., 95s., and even 105s. For the background to the agitation see D. G. Barnes, *A History of the English Corn Laws* (1930).

22. H. Martineau, *op. cit.*, p. 51.

23. W. Smart, *op. cit.*, p. 489. It was not only the "lower

orders" who petitioned against by any means. See A. Briggs, *The Age of Improvement* (1959), p. 201 ff.

24. H. Martineau, *op. cit.*, p. 31.

25. *The Cambridge Chronicle*, 3rd February 1815 and 15th March 1816.

26. 13th March 1816.

27. C. Mackie, *Norfolk Annals* (Norwich 1901), pp. 122, 133.

28. *The Examiner*, 25th December 1814.

29. *The Cambridge Gazette*, 25th November 1815.

30. *The Cambridge Chronicle*, 23rd March 1816.

31. 20th March 1816.

32. 19th March 1816. As the alternative to the Property Tax was indirect taxation, there was more than a little justification for *The Courier's* first contention. See S. Maccoby, *English Radicalism 1786–1832*, Chap. 18, esp. p. 315.

33. *The Cambridge Gazette*, 23rd March 1816.

34. *Ibid.*, 30th March 1816.

35. *The Monthly Review*, July 1816, p. 326.

36. e.g. in *The Times*, 14th March 1816; *Bell's Weekly Messenger*, 17th March 1816; *The Annual Register*, Vol. 58, Part 2, General History; *The New Monthly Magazine*, Vol. 5, May 1816. The whole speech was printed and issued as a pamphlet, *The Speech of Charles Western, Esq., M.P., on the Distressed State of the Agriculture of the Kingdom.*

37. It must be pointed out, however, that rent had been abated by as much as 50 per cent in many places.

38. *Cobbett's Weekly Political Register*, 18th May 1816, also 6th April 1816. In this issue Cobbett deals with the Commons debate on agrarian distress.

39. H. Martineau, *op. cit.*, p. 57.

40. *The Cambridge Chronicle*, 1st March 1816. A petition from Cambridgeshire to the House of Commons mentioned "that in one parish, every proprietor and tenant being ruined with a single exception, the whole poor rates of the parish, thus wholly inhabitated by paupers, are now being paid by an individual whose fortune, once ample, is thus swept entirely away". Quoted in Bovill, *op. cit.*, p. 33.

41. *Bury and Norwich Post*, 13th March 1816.

42. These were William Bell from Southerey, indicted for being involved in the Downham riots who was described as "yeoman" (TS/11/1041/4468), and John Cracknell similarly

described who was charged with armed robbery and riot at Feltwell (Assizes 35/256/Part 1).

CHAPTER FOUR

1. "The man with just a little property found himself driven from employment to make room for those whom the parish must support, yet unless he parted with his property there was no public assistance for him—the parish was rigidly applying a 'means test'." *V. C. H. Cambs.*, *op. cit.*, Vol. 2, p. 97.

2. *New Statesman and Nation*, 4th January 1963. Review of *The Cato Street Conspiracy*, by John Stanhope; and R. J. White, *From Waterloo to Peterloo* (1957), p. 20.

3. Rowley to Sidmouth, 1st March 1816. HO/42/151.

4. Thomas Methwold to Sidmouth, 3rd June 1816. HO/42/151.

5. *The Agricultural State of the Kingdom.*

6. *A full and correct account of the Trials for Rioting at Ely and Littleport, in May 1816, op. cit.* (Preface.)

7. C.R.O.

8. Rowley to Sidmouth, 1st March 1816. HO/42/151.

9. See p. 71.

10. TS/11/1041/4468. For the way the soldiers were dismissed as soon as they were no longer required and for the way they were popularly regarded see Sir John Fortescue, "The Army", in *Johnson's England,* ed. A. S. Turbeville (Oxford, 1952), Vol. 1, Chap. 4.

11. C.R.O.

12. Law to Sidmouth, 27th May 1816. HO/42/150.

13. *Cobbett's Weekly Political Register*, 8th June 1816.

14. Bunbury to Beckett, 26th May 1816. HO/42/150.

15. Grafton to Sidmouth, Bury, 27th May, HO/42/150. Edward Christian also told a Grand Jury at Wisbech the same thing. According to him the trouble was not "the explosion of preconcerted sedition or rebellion, but, deplorable as it was, it was merely the effect of a casual meeting of an idle rabble at an ale house". *Charges delivered to the Grand Juries in the Isle of Ely* (1819, 2nd edit.), p. 8.

16. One article in *The Suffolk Chronicle* (27th April 1816) ascribed the worsening of the poaching war to the return of ex-servicemen who, unable to obtain work, fell in with "the

associates" and brought their military knowledge into play. The gangs it said were usually eighteen to twenty strong and they in turn were met by the gamekeepers in "battle array".

17. Grafton to Sidmouth, Bury, 27th May 1816. HO/42/150.

18. Marrie to Sidmouth, Bildeston, 24th April 1816. HO/42/149.

19. Marrie to Sidmouth, Bildeston, 22nd April 1816. HO/42/149.

20. Marrie to Sidmouth, Bildeston, 25th April 1816. HO/42/149.

21. *The Courier*, 15th, 16th and 17th April 1816. *The Cambridge Chronicle*, 26th April 1816.

22. *Norwich Mercury*, 26th October 1816.

23. *The Star*, 17th March 1817 and 5th April 1817. Clark, who had been imprisoned at Chelmsford, escaped "sans culottes" and was apprehended at Great Dunmow. *Suffolk Chronicle*, 25th January 1817.

24. The one who had turned Crown witness.

25. *The County Chronicle*, 18th March 1817.

26. F. Eden, *op. cit.*

27. *General View ... of Essex*, Vol. 2, p. 396 ff.

28. In the record collection at the Littleport Town Hall.

29. The account books of the Society to 1809 are also in existence.

30. The Articles are in the Cambridge Reference Library. Ref. PAM 47. The scales of relief were as follows:

7s. per week for 6 months when the Club had £40 "at interest".
3s. 6d. per week afterwards when the Club had £40 "at interest".
9s. per week for 3 months when the Club had £80–£150 "at interest".
7s. per week for 3 months when the Club had £80–£150 "at interest".
5s. per week for 3 months when the Club had £80–£150 "at interest".
3s. 6d. per week afterwards when the Club had £80–£150 "at interest".

31. Quoted in *General View ... of Essex*, Vol. 2, p. 396 ff.

32. *Ibid.* Public houses were thick on the ground in these years, and there is no doubt that some relied heavily on the clubs for trade. Colchester, with a population of 8,000, had no less than seventy-five "alehouses". Norwich had 370, and Yar-

mouth, with a population of 13,000, had 137. F. Eden, *op. cit.*

33. *Annals of Agriculture*, Vol. 36, p. 508. Some idea of the quantities of liquor consumed by the labourers might be gleaned from the amount taken by Joseph Bugg before he had enough courage to set fire to the barn of a farmer he loathed, a crime for which he was subsequently executed. According to *The Cambridge Chronicle* he had had a "half quartern of rum, two pints of old beer, five or six pints of other beer, with a half quartern of gin in each". 16th August 1816.

34. Marrie to Sidmouth, 14th May 1816. HO/42/150. On the use of spies in the Luddite districts at this time see F. O. Darvall, *Popular Disturbances and Public Order in Regency England* (1934), Chaps. 13 and 14.

35. K. S. Inglis, *Churches and the Working Classes in Victorian England* (1963), p. 329.

36. *Minutes of the Methodist Conference 1816.*
The numbers of followers in some of the larger places were: Colchester—235. Norwich—700. Thetford—505. Bury St. Edmunds—250. Cambridge—250.

Collections for the Norwich District in 1815 amounted to £534 14s. 9d. See also Maldwyn Edwards, *After Wesley* (1935), Appdx. 1, for a statistical summary of the growth of Methodism between 1789 and 1815.

37. *Norwich Mercury*, 7th September 1816.

38. E. Carter, *History of Cambridgeshire* (1819), p. 66. An extract from the Bishop's Visitation Call Book for 1807 read "*Ely.* Five hundred and sixty houses . . . Service twice, Sacrament first Sunday in the month and on all Festivals to from thirty to forty persons. No Papists. No Dissenters. No Meeting. A few Methodists who have not increased". *Ely Episcopal Records*, p. 54.

39. Townsend, Workman and Eayrs, *A New History of Methodism*, Vol. 1 (1909), Book 3, Chap. 2. J. Petty, *History of the Primitive Methodist Connexion* (1864); H. B. Kendall, *The Origin and History of the Primitive Methodist Church*. See also E. P. Thompson, *op. cit.*, Chap 11 *passim* and E. Hobsbawm, *Primitive Rebels* (1959), Chap. 8.

40. *The Star*, 8th August 1816.

41. Beckett to Sidmouth, 31st May 1816. HO/42/150.

42. See p. 80.

CHAPTER FIVE

1. J. Fyvie, *Notable Dames and Notable Men of the Georgian Era* (1910), Chap. 2.

2. H. Gunning, *Reminiscences of the University, Town and County of Cambridge*, Vol. 2, p. 58 ff. "The last account that reached the University, was that he was seen in '*the basket*' at a cock-pit, the usual punishment for men who made bets which they were unable to pay, as was often the case when luck was against him." Sir Charles Petrie, *The Victorians* (1960), Chap. 8, contains many amusing anecdotes about nineteenth-century clergymen. Spencer Walpole, *op. cit.*, Vol. 1, p. 154, had this to say: "The country squire had other duties to attend to; the country clergyman had nothing to do but shoot or fish. He was frequently the best shot, and the keenest fisherman in the parish. Nothing interfered with his sport except an occasional funeral; and he left the field to read the funeral service with his white surplice barely covering his shooting or hunting dress." Cobbett's opinion of an "average" parson was "that he was an absentee pluralist" who left his work to an "underpaid curate". See e.g. *Rural Rides* 11, p. 96 (Everyman edit.).

3. 25th May 1816.

4. 27th January 1816.

5. *The Cambridge Chronicle*, 14th March 1817.

6. *Returns of Charitable Donations*, 1816.

7. Edward Christian boasted that prior to this period the Isle of Ely had been practically free of crime. *Charges delivered to the Grand Juries in the Isle of Ely, op. cit.* The increase in poaching crimes has been mentioned, there were others. At the Suffolk Assizes in April 1816, for instance, there were thirteen capital convictions for the following: sheep stealing—six; stealing cloth—one; stealing three lambs—one; assault and robbery—two; stealing a colt—one; horse stealing—one; stealing bread and cheese—one. *The Cambridge Chronicle*, 16th April 1816. This is quite typical. The same issue of the *Chronicle* contains a report of the Thetford Assizes where once again stealing food and sheep stealing accounted for most of the capital crimes.

8. 22nd October 1815.

9. Just before the riots began in May, the newspapers were full of descriptions, to the practical exclusion of all else, of the

preparations for the Royal marriage of Princess Charlotte and Prince Leopold. Great details were given of "the nuptials" that must have appeared as a mockery to starving labourers. So too the news that Parliament had voted £60,000 for the Royal establishment, e.g. *The Times*, 22nd March 1816.

10. 12th May 1816. HO/42/150.

11. Cook to Sidmouth, 10th June 1816. HO/42/151.

12. "At Ely, he [Bishop Allen, Bowyer Edward Sparke's successor from 1836] found considerable confusion and uncertainty, in which only one fact was clear, namely, that the leases from which the See drew five-sevenths of its ample revenues had been given on beneficial terms by the late bishop very largely to his relations and henchmen." G. F. A. Best, *Temporal Pillars* (Cambridge 1964) p. 323.

13. *Victoria County History of Cambridgeshire*, Vol. 4, "The Liberty of the Isle in Modern Times," p. 15 ff. The Act repealing the Bishop's jurisdiction is 6 & 7 Will. IV, c.87.

14. Halévy, *England in 1815*, p. 56.

15. *The Cambridge Chronicle*, 3rd March 1815.

16. Marrie to Sidmouth, 25th April 1816. HO/42/149.

17. Wattisham "is worthy of notice for the singular tenure by which the manor is held", wrote Frederick Schoberl. For details of it see *The Beauties of England*, Vol. 14, Part 1, Suffolk, p. 216.

18. Marrie to Sidmouth, 25th April 1816. HO/42/149.

19. C.R.O.

20. Lord Suffield to Sidmouth, 10th June 1816. HO/42/151.

21. *Norwich Mercury*, 7th September 1816.

22. *The Cambridge Chronicle*, 10th May 1816. Many of the newspapers of the time realised that the price increases could lead to trouble and were at pains to point out that the farmers were not responsible. For instance *The London Chronicle,* 10th May 1816: "In consequence of this increased price, the labouring classes in agriculture may think they should have an immediate advance in their wages from the farmer. But they will recollect that in nine cases out of ten the farmer is not benefited by the rise, having sold his Grain before it took place. To feel or execute any ill-will therefore against him for not giving this advance, would be equally unjust and useless. He cannot afford to give it, and those who may attempt to inflame them, or to induce a contrary belief, would only lead them to acts which

could not but be in the highest degree dangerous and even ruinous to themselves."

23. R. J. White, *op cit.*, p. 36.
24. C.R.O. Informations.
25. *Ibid.*
26. *Ibid.*
27. Clapham, *The Economic Journal, op. cit.*, p. 204. M. F. Lloyd Pritchard, *op. cit.*
28. Mackie, *op. cit.*, p. 124. A. M. W. Stirling, *Coke of Norfolk and His Friends* (1912), p. 353 ff. A. D. Bayne, *Royal Illustrated History of Eastern England* (no date), p. 173.
29. Yallop to Sidmouth, 17th May 1816. HO/42/150. The placard was signed with a pointing hand and a heart.
30. *The Courier*, 8th July 1816. The carts were inscribed thus: "Tole End Colliery, Tipton, Staffordshire. Take pity on our children crying for bread. We would rather work than be forced to beg. God restore commerce to our country."
31. Enclosure in Edwards to Sidmouth, 22nd May 1816. HO/42/150.

CHAPTER SIX

1. Mackie, *op. cit.*, p. 122.
2. *The Cambridge Chronicle*, 7th April 1815 and 4th August 1815.
3. *Report from the Select Committee on Petitions Relating to the Corn Laws 1814.* Buxton's evidence.
4. *The Norfolk Chronicle*, 4th March 1815.
5. Appendix: table 12.
6. *The Cambridge Chronicle*, 19th January 1816.
7. Appendix: table 13.
8. Byng to Sidmouth, 7th June 1816. HO/42/151.
9. *General View ... of Norfolk*, p. 63, also J. Evans and J. Britton, *The Beauties of England and Wales*, Vol. 11 (Norfolk).
10. *General View ... of Essex*, Vol. 1, p. 156. *The Colchester Gazette*, 26th October 1816, letter from "A Looker-On".
11. *The Cambridge Chronicle*, 15th March 1816.
12. *Norwich Mercury*, 30th December 1815.
13. *The Cambridge Chronicle*, 17th May 1816. *Bury and Norwich Post*, 15th May 1816.
14. *Bury and Norwich Post*, 17th April 1816.

15. *The Cambridge Chronicle*, etc., 16th August 1816, 30th August 1816.

16. *The Cambridge Gazette*, 27th April 1816.

17. *Bury and Norwich Post*, 2nd April 1817. See *The Cambridge Gazette*, 13th July 1816, for a report of the annual meeting of the Union Fire Insurance Company in Norwich. Great sums had been paid out during the year and some idea of what the state of the countryside was like might be gleaned from the report that 9,000 new members had joined. Thomas Mardley (?) writing to the Home Office about an incident in Lawshall (see p. 76) said that following the discovery of a threatening letter, "I have insured my———4 Houses, 6 calves about 50 coombs of Wheat Barley and Oats . . ." 12th May 1816. HO/42/150.

18. *Bury and Norwich Post*, 24th July 1816. *The Norfolk Chronicle*, 27th July 1816.

19. *General View . . . of Essex*, Vol. 2, p. 197. Also G. E. Fussell, *The Farmer's Tools 1500–1900* (1952).

20. *The Agricultural State of the Kingdom*. Buck was also an opponent of threshing machines, p. 323, ff.

21. *Suffolk Chronicle*, 27th July 1816.

22. Grafton to Sidmouth, 29th April 1816. HO/42/149.

23. See p. 62.

24. Marrie to Sidmouth, 25th April 1816. HO/42/149.

25. *Ibid*. There are no Press reports of a riot at Hitcham.

26. *The Cambridge Chronicle*, 2nd August 1816.

27. Quarter Sessions Records, C.R.O. *The Cambridge Chronicle*, 2nd August 1816. See also appendix : table 6.

28. No true bill was found against Baker. *Bury and Norwich Post*, 29th May 1816. See also appendix : table 4.

29. *The Courier*, 9th May 1816.

30. "I do not hear of one of them stirring in this affair." Marrie to Sidmouth, 25th April 1816. HO/42/149.

31. *Bury and Norwich Post,* 8th May 1816.

32. Thomas Hall to Sidmouth, 13th May 1816. HO/42/150.

33. *The Cambridge Chronicle*, 17th May 1816. Susan Bruty was committed to gaol for firing Shelton's premises and appeared at the Suffolk Assizes in August, but no true bill was found against her. *Bury and Norwich Post*, 26th June and 14th August 1816.

34. Appendix : table 3.

35. Letter from John Gage, 6th May 1816. HO/42/150.

36. Grafton to Sidmouth, 14th May 1816. HO/42/150.

37. *The Star*, 16th May 1816.

38. *The Cambridge Chronicle*, 26th July 1816. *Cambridge Sessions Order Book* (C.R.O.), entries for 19th and 20th July. The Haverhill demonstration is reported in *The Cambridge Gazette*, 18th May 1816. See also appendix : table 8.

39. Sidmouth to Grafton, 24th and 30th April 1816, 2nd May 1816. HO/41/1.

40. Circular by Grafton, dated 1st May 1816. HO/42/150.

41. *Bury and Norwich Post*, 22nd May 1816. *The Morning Post*, 21st May 1816.

42. *The Cambridge Chronicle*, 24th May 1816.

43. *Norwich Mercury*, 8th June 1816. No record of any rioters being brought to trial has been found, although recognizances for William Page, Thomas Pearson, Maurice Row and John Brant to answer indictments for rioting on 16th and 17th May are in the Quarter Sessions file.

44. Actual figures were 1,148 in 1811 and 1,170 in 1821. *Comparative Account: The Population of Great Britain* (1831).

45. F. Schoberl, *op. cit.*

46. The account of the Brandon riots is based on a prosecution brief in the Treasury Solicitor's Papers. Ref. TS/11/940/3381, a few letters in HO/42/150 and 151, and a letter from Moseley, outlining the part he played, in the *Bury and Norwich Post*, 5th June 1816.

47. There are no reports of this anywhere.

48. See later, p. 85.

49. *Ipswich Journal* and *Suffolk Chronicle,* issues of 10th and 17th August 1816, etc.

50. *Ipswich Journal*, 12th April 1817. *The Times*, 10th April 1817. *Bury and Norwich Post*, 9th April 1817. See also appendix : table 7.

CHAPTER SEVEN

1. Yallop (the Mayor of Norwich) to Sidmouth, 17th May 1816. HO/42/150.

2. Account taken from the reports in the *Norwich Mercury* and *The Norfolk Chronicle*. These were reprinted in practically every other newspaper.

3. *The Star*, 3rd June 1816.

4. Yallop to Sidmouth, 7th June 1816. HO/42/151. Yallop to Sidmouth, 31st May 1816. HO/42/150.

5. *Bury and Norwich Post*, 24th July 1816. *The Norfolk Chronicle* and *Norwich Mercury*, 20th July 1816. *The Courier*, 25th July 1816.

6. *The Courier*, 23rd and 25th July 1816. *The Norfolk Chronicle*, 20th July 1816. John Wright to B. Barker, 27th May 1816. HO/42/150. See also appendix : table 10.

7. Barker to Sidmouth, 21st, 24th and 28th May 1816. HO/42/150.

8. *Bury and Norwich Post*, 29th May 1816. *Norwich Mercury*, 25th May 1816.

9. *Norwich Mercury*, 25th May 1816. *The Courier*, 25th May, 1816.

10. Ref. TS/11/1041/4468.

11. *Norwich Mercury*, 24th August 1816.

12. *Ibid*.

13. The details of the Downham Market troubles are also mainly from the Treasury Solicitor's Papers Ref. TS/11/1041/4468; the reports of the trials at the Norfolk and Norwich Assizes in the local Press (dates between 16th and 24th August 1816); and a letter from Lord Suffield to Sidmouth dated 10th June 1816 in HO/42/151.

14. See also the entry in the diary of the Rev. Jeremiah Jackson for 30th May 1816 (in the Wisbech Museum and Literary Institute). "Not a soul at Downham turned out, tho' many were sworn in as constables . . ."

15. Cobbett held forth at great length about "the part, which [had] been acted by the *Yeoman Cavalry*" in the incidents, and coupled them with parsons as among the chief objects of hatred in the countryside, e.g. *Cobbett's Weekly Political Register*, 8th June 1816. Darvall, *op. cit.*, p. 254, however, says that in the North the Yeomanry were not regarded in the same way by the Luddite rioters.

16. See the letter headed "The Late Riots" and signed by "An Eye Witness" in *The Morning Post*, 5th June 1816, in which Lee's troops are praised. Their conduct "may have been equalled, but can never have been exceeded", it said. Suffield's letter in HO/42/151.

17. See p. 51.

18. See also *The Examiner*, 26th May 1816. "We join heartily in condemning the conduct of some Magistrates, who are said

to have entered into terms of compromise with a lawless mob. The certain consequence of such simultaneous and ill-judged conduct must be, as has been found on the present occasion, to increase mischief and disorder."

19 HO/11/2. Transportations Book.

20. HO/47/55.

21. *The Courier* ended a description of the public hanging seen by 10,000 people on Penneden Heath of eight poachers convicted at Maidstone as follows: "After hanging the usual time, and the customary and ridiculous practice of applying the hands of the deceased to children affected with wens, &c., having been performed, the bodies were lowered into shells and coffins, and delivered to their several friends." 2nd September 1816. The practice of touching the bodies was well established in the last decades of the eighteenth century. See J. H. Whiteley, *op. cit.*, p. 164.

22. 7th September 1816. See also the letter signed PHILANTHROPUS objecting on Christian grounds to capital punishment. Thody is spoken of as an inhabitant of both Nacton and Necton in newspaper reports.

CHAPTER EIGHT

1. C.R.O. Except where stated otherwise the narrative of the Ely and Littleport riots is taken from the documents in the Cambridge Record Office. They are of these main types: Prosecution Briefs prepared for the Treasury Solicitors, many with shorthand notes from the trials; letters from magistrates and local solicitors to the Home Office; some statements taken from prisoners; informations laid against the prisoners; bills for witnesses, etc. Duplicates of some of the Prosecution Briefs are also in the Treasury Solicitor's Papers at the Public Record Office. Ref. TS/11/1120/5771.

2. There is a chapter on the Ely and Littleport riots, as local tradition has the story, in W. H. Barrett, *Tales from the Fens* (1963).

3. *The Cambridge Chronicle*, 9th August 1816. The amount is not definite. Later editions of the local Press give a higher figure.

4. *Bury and Norwich Post*, 5th February 1817.

5. *Ibid.*, 12th February 1817. Letter signed "VIATOR".

6. *Ibid.*, 5th March 1817. Letter signed "JUSTITIA".

7. *Ibid.*, 5th March 1817.

8. *Ibid.,* 19th March 1817.

9. The Reverend William James Metcalfe, Rector of Foulmere 1814–50. Brief notes in Joseph Foster, *Index Ecclesiasticus 1800–40* (Oxford, 1890), and J. Venn, *Alumni Cantabrigienses.*

10. Rev. Henry Law, Deacon of Ely, 1804, Rector of Stretham, 1812–18, Rector of Downham. Foster, *op. cit.,* Venn, *op. cit.*

11. Add. MS. 4492. C.U.L.

12. *Ibid.*

13. *Ibid.* Vachell to Law, 2nd June 1816.

14. "It certainly had one effect in sending three fourths of the Littleport rioters home, had they all remained, the disturbances at Ely would have been ten times greater." Vachell to Law, *Ibid.*

15. *The Courier,* 21st June 1816.

16. Law. C.U.L., *op. cit.* Scott to Jones. Downham Market, 26th May 1816. HO/42/150.

17. The Seakins, Hopkin and William Wilson.

CHAPTER NINE

1. G. Pellew, *Life and Correspondence of the Right Honourable Henry Addington, First Viscount Sidmouth* (1847), Vol. 3, p. 145 ff.

2. J. L. Fyvie, *op. cit.,* Chap. 2.

3. See e.g. *The Vauxhall Affray or the Macaronies Defeated* (1773).

4. See e.g. *Adultery. Trial in the Court of King's Bench before Lord Kenyon and a Special Jury between Edward Dodwell, Esq., Plaintiff, and the Rev. Henry Bate Dudley, Defendant, For Crim. Con.*

5. *General View . . . of Essex,* Vol 2, p. 384.

6. *Ibid.,* also R. Wearmouth, *Methodism and the Common People of the Eighteenth Century,* p. 91.

7. J. L. Fyvie, *op. cit.* Also on Bate Dudley see the entries in *The Dictionary of National Biography* and Burke's *Extinct and Dormant Baronetcies of England* (1841) (2nd edit.), p. 175.

8. 24th May 1816. HO/42/150.

9. Bate Dudley to Sidmouth, 24th May 1816. HO/42/150. See the letter signed A LOVER OF JUSTICE in *The Cambridge Chronicle* pointing out that the first blows were struck by Seymour and Daubeny before Bate Dudley even got to Ely. 2nd August 1816.

10. *Ibid.* HO/42/150.

11. Law. C.U.L., *op. cit.*

12. *History of Cambridgeshire*, p. 257.

13. *Ibid.*, p. 258.

14. *The Riots in Cambridgeshire (Littleport and Ely) 1815–16.* "Reprinted from the earliest Records . . .", p. 3.

15. Bate Dudley to Sidmouth, 31st May 1816. HO/42/150.

16. *The Cambridge Chronicle,* 11th April 1817. There are no Press reports of an attack on Garratt's shop, but a note at the Cambridgeshire Record Office said that Jessop was involved in something there. The case was not proceeded with.

17. "At a Vestry meeting held this day at the vestry room it was agreed to submit to the consideration of the Magistrates the propriety of purchasing a Life Annuity of £5 p^r annum or of paying £5 annually, out of the Poor Rates, for the Permanent relief of a private in the 1st Regiment of Guards, who recieved [*sic*] a wound in his Arm of the 24th of May last in the suppression of the rioters at Littleport,—to be paid him Quarterly." Entry for 3rd December 1816 in the Littleport Vestry Records.

18. *The British Volunteer,* 6th July 1816.

19. The depositions before the Coroner are in HO/42/150.

20. Bate Dudley to Sidmouth, 31st May 1816. HO/42/150.

21. 31st May 1816. Both the Rev. Jeremiah Jackson and James Peck wrote in their diaries (both in the Wisbech Museum and Literary Institute) that *three* were killed. Jackson, for instance, wrote "At Littleport three of the rioters and one soldier, a Waterloo man killed . . ." Entry for 24th May.

22. W. H. Barrett, *op. cit.*, p. 91.

23. Law. C.U.L., *op. cit.*

24. 8th June 1816.

25. Law to Sidmouth, Ely, 27th May 1816. HO/42/150.

26. On the hiring of Bow Street Officers, etc., see L. Radzinowicz, *History of English Criminal Law*, Vol. 2, pp. 258 ff and 261, f.n. 16.

27. Sidmouth refused to allow the Brandon magistrates to hire a Bow Street Officer. Sidmouth to Burch and Moseley, 19th May 1816. HO/41/1.

28. He would not agree to Special Assizes for Norfolk and Suffolk. Sidmouth to Grafton, 4th June 1816. HO/41/1.

29. Sidmouth to Yallop, 18th May 1816. HO/41/1.

30. Sidmouth to Burch and Moseley, 19th May 1816. HO/41/1.

31. Sidmouth to Metcalfe and Law, 24th May 1816. HO/41/1.

32. *The Hue and Cry and Police Gazette,* 8th June 1816. *Bury and Norwich Post,* 29th May 1816.

33. Beckett to Captain Buckley, 15th August 1816. HO/41/1.

34. *Norwich Mercury,* 1st June 1816.

35. *Bury and Norwich Post,* 29th May 1816.

CHAPTER TEN

1. The details of the Upwell riots are again taken mainly from the uncatalogued papers in the Cambridgeshire Record Office. The Bowers referred to is not the person mentioned on pp. 88–9. According to one witness it was really Robert Lancaster.

2. One of whom was a bricklayer who had been earning 15s. a week throughout the winter. *The Cambridge Gazette,* 25th May 1816.

3. Rowley to Sidmouth, 1st June 1816. HO/42/151, and a letter from a Huntingdon magistrate dated 24th May 1816 in HO/42/150. *The Cambridge Chronicle,* 9th August 1816. *The Cambridge Gazette,* 10th August 1816.

4. *The Courier,* 27th May, 1816.

5. *The Cambridge Gazette,* 8th June 1816. Letter signed "An Impartial Observer".

6. *The Cambridge Chronicle,* 31st May 1816. *Bury and Norwich Post,* 29th May 1816.

7. *Cobbett's Weekly Political Register,* 8th June 1816. *The Courier,* 27th May 1816.

8. *The Courier,* 7th June 1816, and letters dated 30th and 31st May 1816 in HO/42/150.

9. Bunbury to Beckett, 26th May 1816. HO/42/150. Grafton had heard the same story. See Grafton to Sidmouth, 25th May 1816. HO/42/150.

10. Magistrates of Wisbech to Sidmouth, 23rd and 26th May 1816. HO/42/150. Also entries for 25th, 26th and 27th May 1816 in the diary of the Rev. Jeremiah Jackson and 25th May 1816 in the diary of John Peck.

11. *The Courier,* 29th May 1816. W. Watson, *An Historical Account of the Ancient Town and Port of Wisbech* (Wisbech 1827), pp. 398–401.

BREAD OR BLOOD 163

12. *Cobbett's Weekly Political Register,* 8th June 1816.

13. Byng to Sidmouth, 7th June 1816. HO/42/151. *The Star,* 25th May 1816. *Suffolk Chronicle,* 25th May 1816.

14. Grafton to Sidmouth, 5th June 1816. HO/42/151.

15. Letter dated 10th June 1816. HO/42/151.

16. Sidmouth to Grafton, 28th May 1816. HO/41/1.

17. Sidmouth to Suffield, 4th June 1816. HO/41/1.

18. Evans to Hobhouse, 5th June 1816. HO/42/151. The Treasury Solicitors Office at this period arranged all official prosecutions. For a description of the whole process see Darvall, *op. cit.,* Chap 12, "The Machinery of Order".

19. Sidmouth to Barker, 27th May 1816, Sidmouth to Byng, 1st June 1816. HO/41/1.

20. HO/42/151.

CHAPTER ELEVEN

1. Sidmouth to the Bishop of Ely, 11th June 1816. HO/41/1.

2. Sidmouth to Byng, 30th May and 12th June 1816. HO/41/1.

3. C.R.O. There is a letter in HO/42/151 dated 17th June 1816, however, stating Abbott's complaints about the court-room. They were so draughty, he said, as to cause blindness (!).

4. *Ibid.*

5. E. Foss, *The Judges of England* (1870), Lord Campbell, *Lives of the Chief Justices* (1849), *Dictionary of National Biography.*

6. *Mr. Justice Abbott's charge to the Grand Jury before the Honourable Mr. Justice Burrough and Edward Christian, Esq. (Copied from Mr. Gurney's shorthand notes),* (Ely, 1816).

7. E. Foss, *op. cit.*; *D.N.B.*; Lord Campbell, *op. cit.*; Townshend, *Twelve Judges.*

8. H. Gunning, *op. cit.,* Vol. 1, pp. 192–200; *D.N.B.*; C. H. Cooper, *Annals of Cambridge* (Cambridge, 1854), Vol. 4, pp. 432, 468.

9. p. 200.

10. "Wednesday" (no date) HO/42/151. Christian had also been the moving spirit behind "the enactment of 1792, which expressly forbade any magistrate to issue a vagrant pass until the bearer had either been whipped or imprisoned for at least seven days". *V.C.H., Cambs.,* Vol. 2, p. 103.

11. 6th July 1816. HO/42/152. There had been numerous widely distributed Press reports to the effect that Christian was to be ignored. For instance, "The Special Commission to try the Ely rioters has passed the Great Seal", *The Manchester Mercury* reported on 11th June. "The judicial authority vested by Charter in the Chief Justice of that Isle will thus be superseded."

12. 6th July 1816. HO/42/152.

13. See also *V.C.H., Cambs.*, Vol. 4, pp. 19–20.

14. 31st May 1816.

15. *The Monthly Repository*, Vol. 11, May 1816, p. 307. Presumably this refers to the sentiments in Bacon's Essay on "Revenge". "Public revenges are for the most part fortunate; as that for the death of Caesar . . . But in private revenge, it is not."

16. E. Coneybeare, *op. cit.*, p. 258.

17. 21st June 1816. The sermon was eventually published as *A Sermon delivered at the Cathedral of Ely on Monday the 17th June 1816 before Mr. Justice Abbott, Mr. Justice Burrough and Chief Justice Christian on the Opening of their Special Commission for the trial of the rioters* (Cambridge, 1816).

18. Criminal Register 1816. HO/27/12.

19. *Cobbett's Weekly Political Register*, 22nd June 1816.

20. HO/42/150.

21. Bollard to Beckett, 19th June 1816. HO/42/151.

22. Bollard to Beckett, 20th June 1816. HO/42/151. The actual incidents and the labourers charged with them are detailed in all the newspapers and reprinted in Johnson, *op. cit.*

23. Littleport Vestry Records, *op. cit.* Entry for 14th June.

24. These included some charged for the Upwell and Outwell incidents.

25. Prosecution Brief King v. Henry Benson. C.R.O.

26. For instance, he said that Thody, the Downham Market rioter, led the march to Ely, and that Peploe Ward was told three days before the riot that the Littleport people intended to go to Ely.

27. Evans to ?, 28th January 1817. TS/11/1027/4353.

28. Richard Cooper the elder, and Richard Cooper the younger, were traversed on a charge of rioting.

29. Hobhouse to Evans, Lincoln's Inn, 30th January 1817. C.R.O.

30. Abbott's address to the prisoners is printed in full in *The Hue and Cry and Police Gazette*, 29th June 1816.

31. The total number of prisoners was seventy-six. Apart from

the twenty-four condemned to death as above, five were acquitted, ten discharged by proclamation, one convicted of larceny and thirty-six were on bail on their good behaviour.

32. Letter announcing the decision signed by Abbott and Burrough 27th June 1816 in *Circuit Letters and Judges and Justices Recommendations.* HO/6/1.

33. Letter from Robert Hardwicke, Cambridge, 8th June 1816. C.R.O. Also Home Office Entry Book. HO/13/28.

34. These were Robert Crabbe, Aaron Layton, William Atkin, John Cooper, William Dann, Sarah Hobbes, John Pricke, James Cammell, Christopher Butcher, William Beamiss junior.

35. The address has been quoted before and it is reprinted as Chap. 17 in Christian's *Charges delivered to the Grand Juries in the Isle of Ely.*

36. Letter dated 25th June 1816. HO/41/1

37. Letter from Evans to ?, Ely. TS/11/1041/4468. The gallows were at the Mill Pits, "near a pathway leading behind the workhouse". *Chronicles of Littleport,* R. T. Sonley. MSS. work of little interest in the Littleport Town Hall records. Hitherto executions had been from a cart, in a way approved of by Dr. Johnson. The prisoner had a noose put round his neck and the cart was driven from under him, like Tom Jones.

38. *The Cambridge Chronicle,* 5th July 1816.

39. *The Courier,* 1st July 1816.

40. *The Cambridge Chronicle,* 5th July 1816.

41. *The Cambridge Gazette,* 6th July 1816.

42. 3rd August 1816. There is a stone slab on the west buttress of the south side of St. Mary's Church bearing an inscription commemorating the burials. Sonley said the bodies were laid in a cottage "in Gaol Street (next to the opening leading to the back of *The Bell Hotel*)", *op. cit.*

43. *The Cambridge Chronicle,* 5th July 1816.

44. Letter from Evans, 28th June 1816. HO/42/151. The "confession" was published in every newspaper consulted.

45. See e.g. *The Cambridge Chronicle,* 26th July 1816, and letters signed "A LOVER OF JUSTICE" and "ELIENSIS" in the issue of 2nd August 1816. Also *The Courier,* 26th July and 9th August 1816, and *The Cambridge Gazette,* 17th August 1816, letter signed "THE ASSOCIATES".

46. *Bury and Norwich Post,* 4th June 1817.

47. HO/6/1.

48. *Bury and Norwich Post,* 17th July 1816.

49. Bate Dudley to Evans, Sloane Square, 1st July 1816. C.R.O.

50. Letter dated 24th June 1816. C.R.O.

51. The first fleet to Botany Bay sailed in 1787.

52. *The Cambridge Chronicle,* 21st July 1815. See the report of Kirkby v. Jackson in the Nisi Prius Court. There was a Botany Bay farm, near March, mentioned in the trial.

53 *Report from the Select Committee on Secondary Punishments 1831,* p. 110. See also the evidence of T. G. B. Estcourt, Dr. G. Rutherford and John Henry Capper. The novel by Marcus Clarke, *For the Term of His Natural Life,* is based on official records.

54. 24th March 1816.

55. Transportations Book. HO/11/2.

56. Barker to Sidmouth, 25th June 1816. HO/42/151. The Bill read "A caution for Worlington farmers that youre the threshen meshien for whe are determined to seet fire to everyone that comes to Worlington and if the remainer part are not made away with we will fire the Bilding whare whare it is in".

57. Letter dated 26th June 1816. HO/42/151.

58. *The Cambridge Gazette,* 28th August 1816.

59. *Bury and Norwich Post,* 30th October 1816. *Ipswich Journal,* 19th October 1816. *Suffolk Chronicle,* 19th October 1816. *The Colchester Gazette,* 26th October 1816.

60. *Ipswich Journal,* 26th October 1816. *The Norfolk Chronicle,* 2nd November 1816.

61. *Bury and Norwich Post,* 29th January 1817. Sessions Book—Bury Quarter Sessions, Epiphany 1817 (County Record Offices, Ipswich), See also appendix : table 9.

62. *Norwich Mercury,* 17th December 1816.

63. *The Cambridge Chronicle,* 13th September 1816.

64. *Victoria County History of Norfolk,* Vol. 2, p. 524. Mackie, *op. cit.*

65. *Report from Her Majesty's Commissioners for inquiring into the Administration and Practical operation of the Poor Laws* (1834), Supplement No. 1, Vol. 1, pp. 56–65. See also "Captain Swing in East Anglia", A. J. Peacock (wrongly accredited) in *The Bulletin of the Society for the Study of Labour History,* June 1964.

BIBLIOGRAPHY

BIBLIOGRAPHY

1. *Newspapers and Journals consulted*
    Annual Register, The
    Bell's Weekly Messenger
    British Review, The
    British Volunteer, The
    Bury and Norwich Post
    Cambridge Chronicle, The
    Cambridge Gazette, The
    Christian Observer, The
    Cobbett's Weekly Political Register
    Colchester Gazette, The
    County Chronicle, The
    Courier, The
    Essex Herald, The
    Examiner, The
    Gentlemen's Magazine, The

    Hue and Cry and Police Gazette, The
    Ipswich Journal
    London Chronicle, The
    Manchester Mercury, The
    Monthly Repository, The
    Monthly Review, The
    Morning Post, The
    New Monthly Magazine, The
    Norfolk Chronicle, The
    Norwich Mercury
    Pamphleteer, The
    Star, The
    Suffolk Chronicle
    Times, The

2. *Documents relating to the riots etc., consulted*
    Treasury Solicitor's Papers (Public Record Office)
        Ref. Nos. TS/11/940/3381
                  TS/11/1027/4353
                  TS/11/1041/4468
                  TS/11/1120/5771

    Home Office Papers (Public Record Office)
    Ref. Nos. HO/6/1
              HO/11/2
              HO/13/28
              HO/27/12
              HO/38
              HO/40/(1-8)
              HO/41/1

    Ref. Nos. HO/42/148
              HO/42/149
              HO/42/150
              HO/42/151
              HO/42/152
              HO/47/55

    Assize Records (Public Record Office) Ref. Assizes 35/256/Part 1
    Documents on the Ely and Littleport riots (Cambridgeshire Record Office)
        uncatalogued
    Letters on the Ely and Littleport riots by Henry Law (Cambridge University
        Library) Ref. ADD. MS. 4492
    Cambridge Quarter Sessions Records (Cambridgeshire Record Office)
    East Suffolk Quarter Sessions Records (Ipswich Record Office)
    West Suffolk Quarter Sessions Records (Bury St. Edmund's Record Office)
    Norwich Assembly Book (Norfolk and Norwich Record Office)
    Papers relating to Suffolk (British Museum Ref. 10351 i 10)
    Cuttings from newspapers etc., relating to Suffolk (British Museum Ref.
        10351 i 9)
    Diary of the Rev. Jeremiah Jackson (Wisbech Museum and Literary Institute)
    Diary of John Peck, Parson Drove (Wisbech Museum and Literary Institute)
    Sonley MSS (Littleport Town Hall)

3. *Early accounts of the riots etc.*
    Bereton, C. D.   *An Inquiry into the Workhouse System and the Laws of
                            Maintenance in Agricultural Districts.* (Norwich, no
                            date, possibly 1825)

Christian, E.   *Charges delivered to the Grand Juries in the Isle of Ely.* 2nd. edit. (1819)

    „   „   *A vindication of the Common Law and the administration of Public Justice in England from the imputation of cruelty.* (1819)

—   *The Vauxhall Affray or the Macaronis defeated.* (1773)

—   *Adultery. Trial in the Court of King's Bench before Lord Kenyon and a special Jury between Edward Dodwell, Esq., Plaintiff, and the Rev. Henry Bate Dudley, Defendant, for Crim. Con.* (1789)

—   *A full and correct account of the Trials and Rioting at Ely and Littleport in May, 1816.* (1816)

—   *Trials of the Prisoners at the Isle of Ely Special Assizes.* (Cambridge 1816)

—   *The Trials of the Rioters at Littleport and Ely with their Several Sentences.* (Bury St. Edmunds, no date, presumably 1816)

4. *Government reports etc.*

—   *The Agricultural State of the Kingdom* (1816)

Vancouver, C.   *General View of the Agriculture of the County of Cambridgeshire* (1794)

Gooch, W.   *General View* . . . . *Cambridgeshire* (1813)

Stone, T.   *General View* . . . . *Huntingdon* (1793)

Parkinson, R.   *General View* . . . . *Huntingdon* (1811)

Young, A.   *General View* . . . . *Essex* (2 vols) (1807)

    „   „   *General View* . . . . *Suffolk* (1797)

    „   „   *General View* . . . . *Norfolk* (1804)

Kent, N.   *General View* . . . . *Norfolk* (1796)

Marshall, W.   *The Rural Economy of Norfolk* (1795)

—   *Annals of Agriculture*

Young, A.   *Inquiry into the Propriety of Applying Wastes to the Better Maintenance and Support on the Poor.* (1801)

—   *Report from the Committee on the Nature and Effect of the Game Laws.* (1816)

—   *Report from the Select Committee on Petitions Relating to the Corn Laws.* (1814)

—   *Report from the Select Committee on the Poor Laws.* (1817)

—   *Report from the Select Committee on the Poor Laws.* (1818)

—   *Report from Her Majesty's Commissioners for inquiring into the Administration and Practical Operation of the Poor Laws.* (1834)

—   *Extracts from the Information received by Her Majesty's Commissioners as to the Administration and Operation of the Poor Laws.* (1837)

—   *Report from the Select Committee on Labourers' Wages.* (1824)

—   *Report from the Select Committee on Secondary Punishments.* (1831)

—   *Report from the Select Committee on Criminal Commitments and Convictions.* (1827)

—   *Returns of Charitable Donations 1786-8.* (1816)

—   *Minutes of the Methodist Conference 1816.*

5. *Articles quoted*

Hobsbawm, E.   "The Machine Breakers", *Past and Present*, Vol. 1. (1952)

Chambers, J. D.   "Enclosure and Labour Supply in the Industrial Revolution", *Economic History Review*, Vol. 5, 1952-3.

Clapham, J.   "The Transference of the Worsted Industry from Norfolk to the West Riding", *Economic Journal*, Vol. 20, 1910

Fussell, G. E. &
  Compton, M.   "Agricultural Adjustments after the Napoleonic
                        Wars", *Economic History* supplement of *The Econo-
                        mic Journal*, Vol. 3, No. 14, February 1939
Fussell, G. E. &
  Goodman, C.   "Housing of the Rural Population in the Eighteenth
                        Century", *Economic History* supplement of *The
                        Economic Journal*, Vol. 2, No. 5, January 1930
Gash, N.   "Rural Unemployment, 1815-34", *Economic History
                        Review*, Vol. 6, No. 1, October 1935
Lloyd Pritchard, M. F. "The Decline of Norwich", *Economic History Review*,
                        2nd series, Vol. 3, No. 3, 1951
Glover, G.   "Observation on the State of Pauperism", *The
                        Pamphleteer*, Vol. 10, No. 20, 1817
Peter, W.   "Thoughts on the Present Crisis", *The Pamphleteer*,
                        Vol. 8, No. 15, 1816
Smart, W.   "Antecedents of the Corn Law of 1815", *English
                        Historical Review*, Vol. 24, 1909
Davies, E.   "The small landowner, 1780-1832 in the light of the
                        Land Tax Assessments", *Economic History Review*,
                        Vol. 1, January 1927

6. *Secondary sources*
Allison, R. Archibald   *Lives of Lord Castlereagh and Sir C. Stewart.* (1861)
Archer, G. L.   *Old Ely.* (Ely 1949)
Ashton, T. S.   *An Economic History of England in the 18th Century.*
                        (1955)
Bamford, Samuel   *Passages in the Life of a Radical.* (1844) 2 vols
Barnes, D. G.   *A History of the English Corn Laws.* (1930)
Barrett, W. H.   *Tales from the Fens.* (1963)
Bayne, A. D.   *Royal Illustrated History of Eastern England.* (no date)
Bayne-Powell, R.   *English Country Life in the Eighteenth Century.* (1937)
Best, G. F. A.   *Temporal Pillars.* (Cambridge 1964)
Bovill, E. W.   *English Country Life 1780-1830.* (1962)
Briggs, A.   *The Age of Improvement.* (1959)
Brown, A. F. J.   *English History from Essex Sources.* (Chelmsford 1952)
Carter, E.   *History of Cambridgeshire.* (1819)
Clapham, J. H.   *An Economic History of Modern Britain.* "The Early
                        Railway Age". (1950)
Coneybeare, E.   *History of Cambridgeshire.* (1897)
Cooper, C. H.   *The Annals of Cambridge.* (5 Vols. 1842-1908)
Cromwell, T.   *History of Colchester.* (Colchester 1825)
Curtler, W. H. R.   *The Enclosure and Redistribution of Our Land.* (Oxford
                        1920)
Darvall, F. O.   *Popular Disturbances and Public Order in Regency
                        England.* (1934)
Day, J. Wentworth   *A History of the Fens.* (1954)
Eden, Sir F. M.   *A State of the Poor.* (abridged ed. A. G. L. Rogers
                        1928)
Edwards, Maldwyn   *After Wesley.* (1935)
Ernle, Lord   *English Farming Past and Present.* (6th ed. 1961)
Evans, J. & Britton, J. *The Beauties of England.* Vol. 11. (Norfolk) (1810)
Fay, C. R.   *Life and Labour in the Nineteenth Century.* (1933)
Fussell, G. E.   *The Farmer's Tools.* (1952)
     „   *The English Rural Labourer.* (1947)
Fyvie, J. L.   *Notable Dames and Notable Men of the Georgian Era.*
                        (1910)
George, M. D.   *England in Transition.* (Pelican 1962)
Gunning, H.   *Reminiscences of the University, Town and County of
                        Cambridge.* 2 Vols. (2nd edit. 1855)
Halévy, E.   *History of the English People in 1815.* (Penguin edition
                        1937)
Hammond, J. L. & B.   *The Village Labourer.* (1911)

Hampson, E.   *Treatment of Poverty in Cambridgeshire.* (1934)
Hasbach, W.   *History of the English Agricultural Labourer.* (1908)
Hobsbawm, E.   *Primitive Rebels.* (1959)
Inglis, K. S.   *Churches and the Working Class in Victorian England.* (1963)
Johnson, A. H.   *The Disappearance of the Small Landowner.* (Oxford 1909)
Johnson, C.   *An account of the Ely and Littleport Riots in 1816.* (Ely 1893)
Kendall, H. B.   *The Origin and History of the Primitive Methodist Church.* (1906)
Knight, C.   *Popular History of England*, Vol. 8
Mackie, Charles   *Norfolk Annals.* (Norwich 1901)
Marshall, Dorothy   *English People in the Eighteenth Century.* (1956)
     ,,   ,,   *Eighteenth Century England.* (1962)
Maccoby, Simon   *English Radicalism 1786-1832.* (1955)
Martineau, Harriet   *A History of the Thirty Years' Peace*
Mingay, G. E.   *English Landed Society in the Eighteenth Century.* (1963)
Pellew, G.   *Life and Correspondence of the Right Honourable Henry Addington, First Viscount Sidmouth.* (1847)
Petty, J.   *History of the Primitive Methodist Connexion.* (1864)
Radzinowicz, L.   *History of English Criminal Law.* (1948 and 1956)
Raven, J. J.   *History of Suffolk.* (1895)
Redford, A.   *Labour Migration in England.* (2nd edit. 1963)
Schoberl, F.   *The Beauties of England*, Vol. 14. (Suffolk) (1813)
Stirling, A. M. W.   *Coke of Norfolk and His Friends.* (1912)
Taylor, J.   *The Age We Live In, A History of the XIXth Century* (no date)
Thompson, E. P.   *The Making of the English Working Class.* (1963)
Townsend, W. J.,
   Workman, H. B.,
   & Eayrs, G.   *A New History of Methodism*, Vol. 1. (1909)
Walpole, Spencer   *A History of England.* (1913)
Watson, J. Steven   *The Reign of George III. 1760-1815.* (Oxford 1960)
Watson, W.   *An Historical Account of the Ancient Town and Port of Wisbech.* (Wisbech 1827)
Wearmouth, R.   *Methodism and the Common People of the Eighteenth Century.* (1945)
     ,,   ,,   *Methodism and the Working Class Movements of England.* (1937)
Webb, S. & B.   *English Poor Law History.* Vol. 1. (1927)
White, R. J.   *From Waterloo to Peterloo.* (1957)
     ,,   *Life in Regency England.* (1964)
Whiteley, J. H.   *Wesley's England.* (1954)
—   *A topographical and historical account of the City and County of Norwich.* (1819)
—   *The Riots in Cambridgeshire (Ely and Littleport) 1815-16.* "Reprinted from the earlier records, for R.A., a country gentleman". (Ely 1890)
—   *Victoria County History of Cambridgeshire* Vols. 2 and 4
                 ,,   ,,   ,,   *Huntingdonshire* Vol. 2.
                 ,,   ,,   ,,   *Essex*, Vol. 2
                 ,,   ,,   ,,   *Suffolk*, Vol. 2
                 ,,   ,,   ,,   *Norfolk*, Vol. 2

7. *Reference books*
Campbell, Lord   *Lives of the Chief Justices.* (1849)
Foss, E.   *The Judges of England.* (1870)
Foster, J.   *Index Ecclesiasticus 1800-40.* (1890)
Venn, J.   *Alumni Cantabrigienses*
Burke's *Extinct and Dormant Baronetcies of England.* (2nd ed. 1841)
Dictionary of National Biography
The Clerical Guide

APPENDIX

TABLES

A—Name of Labourer
B—Married or Single
C—Village
D—Occupation
E—Number of Offences
F—Remarks
G—Number of Children
H—Average weekly earnings
I—Weekly allowance from Parish

TABLE 1

Names of Labourers involved in incidents at Ely and Littleport

A.	B.	C.	D.	E.	F.	G.	H.	I.
1. Wm. Atkin		Ely		2		4		
2. Wm. Beamiss sen.	(M)	Littleport		4				
3. Wm. Beamiss jun.	(S)	,,		3				
4. Christopher Butcher		,,	Shoemaker	1			4/–	
5. John Burridge	(S)	,,	Labourer	2		1	£1	
6. Richard Burridge	(M)	,,	,,	1		1	£1	
7. Mark Benton	(M)	,,	,,	2				
8. Hy. Benson	(M)	,,	Farmer	1	Claimed authorship			
9. Rich. Burridge	(M)	,,	Labourer	5				
10. James Cammell		Ely	,,	3		3		
11. Hy. Chapman		,,	,,	2				
12. Aaron Chevell	(M)	Littleport	,,	4		5	15/–	
13. Robt. Crabb	(M)	,,	,,	2		2	10/–	
14. Jarvis Cranwell	(M)	,,	,,	1				
15. Rich. Cooper		Ely	No occupation	1	Riot at Ely. Very active			
16. John Cooper		Ely	Brickmaker	1	,, ,,			
17. Rich. Cooper jun.		Ely	No occupation	1	,, ,,			
18. Geo. Crow	(M)	Littleport	Labourer	3			8/–	
19. John Dennis	(M)	,,	Victualler	3 at least				
20. Wm. Dann	(M)	Littleport	Labourer	3		5	15/–	2/–
21. Thos. Dobbs	(M)	,,	,,	1		2	12/–	
22. Thos. Dench		Ely	Labourer	1				
23. Joseph Easey	(M)	Littleport	,,	3		1	9/–	

No.	Name		Place	Occupation		Remarks			
24.	John Easey	(M)	Ramsey	Waterman	2		1	9/–	
25.	Thos. Edgerley	(M)	Littleport	Labourer	1		3	14/–	
26.	John Freeman	(M)	,,	,,	1		4	12/–	6d
27.	John Gaultrip	(M)	,,	,,	1		3	12/–	4/6
28.	Thos. Gray	(S)	,,	Shoemaker	2			9/–	
29.	John Green	(M)	,,	Labourer	1			9/–	
30.	Wm. Gotobed			,,	1				
31.	Thos. Gotobed		(No place)		1	Not apprehended			
32.	Wm. Greaves		Downham	Labourer	2				
33.	Flanders Hopkin	(M)	Littleport	,,	1				
34.	Thos. Hunt		Ely	Tailor	1	Very active	4	9/–	2/6
35.	John Hunt	(M)	Littleport	Labourer	1		2	9/–	
36.	Isaac Harley jun.		Ely	,,	3				
37.	Sarah Hobbes		Downham		1	Not apprehended			
38.	Joseph Hopkin				1				
39.	John Hassett	(M)	Littleport	"Irishman"	6				
40.	Richard Jessop		,,	Labourer	1	Bail	1	9/–	
41.	Joseph Irons	(M)	,,	,,	1	Bailed	3	14/–	
42.	John Lee		Ely	,,	2				
43.	Aaron Layton	(M)	Littleport	Bricklayer	1		3	10/–	8d
44.	Jos. Lavender	(M)	,,	Labourer	1		1	9/–	
45.	Wm. Murfitt	(S)	,,	,,	4			6/–	
46.	Hy. Mainer	(M)	,,	Shoemaker	1			9/–	
47.	John Morris	(M)	,,	Labourer	1				
48.	Philip Morris	(S)	,,	,,	1				
49.	Elizabeth Newman	(S)	,,	Single woman	1	Active	1	9/–	5/–
50.	Robt. Nicholas	(S)	,,	Labourer	1			8/–	
51.	Jas. Newell	(S)	,,	,,	2			6/–	
52.	Rich. Nicholas	(S)	,,	,,	1			9/–	
53.	Robt. Porter	(S)	,,	Potter	1			9/–	
54.	John Pricke	(M)	Ely	Labourer	1	Treasurer			
55.	Rich. Rutter	(M)	Littleport	,,	1	Occupier of land of his own	1	12/–	
56.	Stephen Rowell	(M)	,,		1		3		
57.	Brassett Rayner	(M)	,,	Shopkeeper	1				1/6

TABLE 1—*continued*

A.	B.	C.	D.	E.	F.	G.	H.	I.
58. Joseph Stibbard	(S)	,,	Labourer	1	Chelsea Pensioner		8/-	
59. Samuel Seakins		Downham	Labourer	1				
60. Matthew Seakins		,,	,,	1				
61. Thos. Seakins	(S)	,,	,,	10	Refused to work for 9/-			
62. Thos. South jun.*		Littleport	Labourer				6/-	
63. Robert Salmon	(S)	,,	,,	3	Cottage & garden		10/-	
64. Wm. Sibley	(M)	,,	Carpenter	1	Secreting rioters	2	15/-	
65. David Stimson				1	Crown witness			
66. John Sparrow								
67. John South	(S)	,,	Labourer				6/-	
68. John Jefferson	(S)				"Independent of extra earnings"			
69. Wm. Jefferson	(S)						9/-	
70. Robt. Porter son of Joshua	(S)						9/-	
71. Francis Torrington	(S)	,,	Shoemaker	1	Pension—Marine service		6/-	1/3
72. Jas. Wortley	(M)	,,	Labourer	1		4	10/-	
73. Wm. Walker	(S)	Downham	,,	2			8/-	
74. Wm. Wilson		Ely	,,	2			12/-	
75. John Walton		Downham		1				
76. John Wilson			Shoemaker	1				
77. Daniel Wilson	(M)	Littleport	Blacksmith	2	In business for himself	3		
78. John Warner	(M)		Labourer	1	House & garden		9/-	
79. Wilson Wyebrow	(M)	,,				1	9/-	
80. John Walker	(M)	,,	,,		Cottage & garden	3	10/-	

* South left his job of Rod cutting at which he could have earned 15/- per week in consequence of which, on his applying to the Overseers for work, he received only 8d. per day.

N.B. The above statement is in general beneath the weekly earnings of the families of the Prisoners, as in many cases the earnings of the women and children could not be ascertained.

(This list with a few additions is a copy of a document drawn up for the Treasury Solicitors, in the Cambridge Record Office)

TABLE 2

Names of Labourers involved in riots at Downham Market, 21st May 1816

Name	Age	Village	Occupation	Sentence
John Stern	33	Southerey	Labourer	7 years transportation
John Bowers		,,	,,	*
Daniel Elmer		,,	,,	
William Bell	41	,,	Yeoman	14 years transportation*
Gamaliel Porter		,,	Labourer	
John Neal		,,	,,	
William Hardy		,,	,,	
Elijah Piggott		,,	,,	
Joseph Grimmer		,,	,,	
James Goat		,,	,,	
James Galley		,,	,,	
Joseph Ricket		,,	,,	
Joseph Campbell		,,	,,	
John Terry		Downham Market	,,	
John Skinn		,,	,,	
Thomas Thody	25	,,	,,	Death. Executed
Charles Nelson		,,	,,	Transportation for life*
Harrison Bone		,,	,,	
Lucy Rumbelow		,,		6 months hard labour*
Amelia Lightharness	23	,,		Transportation for life*
Elizabeth Watson	49	,,		1 year hard labour*
Hannah Jarvis	36	,,	Widow	Transportation for life*
Margaret Jerry	33	,,		1 year hard labour*
John Pearson		,,		*
William English		,,		
John Milk		,,		
William Fendike		,,	Labourer	
Elizabeth King		,,		1 year hard labour*
Frances Parker		,,		*
James (or William) Galley		,,		1 year hard labour
Mary Scott		,,		
William Young		Hilgay	Labourer	1 year hard labour*
Sarah Moore	17	,,	Labouring woman	No true Bill
Spencer Rayner		Downham Market	Labourer	(Not taken)
James Goatlake		Hilgay	,,	
Edward Wilson			Blacksmith	
John Blogg		Downham Market		*
John Bell		,,		
Francis Porter		,,		
Daniel Harwood		,,	Labourer	Executed
Edward Miller				
William Galley				
Edward Millon				*

* Commuted from the death sentence.

TABLE 3

Labourers charged with breaking threshing machine belonging to J. Wakes at Stoke by Clare—9th May 1816
(Bury Quarter Sessions—August 1816)

Thos. Meers	12 months	James Swallow	Discharged
Stephen Clark	,, ,,	John Deeks	,,
Geo. Farrant sen. (or Farrance)	,, ,,	Sarah Jackson	,,
Mary Jackson	,, ,,	George Atterton	,,
Richard Rogers	,, ,,	James Angell	,,
Geo. Farrant jun.	6 months	William Turner	,,
William Jackson	,, ,,	C. Meers	,,
George Frost	3 months		

TABLE 4

Labourers charged with breaking Samuel or John Fenton's threshing tackle at Welnetham

Jacob Halls	13 months	Henry Atterton	9 months
Samuel Grindley	,, ,,	William Robinson	not guilty
Rhinaldo Barcham	,, ,,		

TABLE 5

Labourers charged with destroying threshing tackle the property of Thomas Kemp—Sunday 19th May
(Bury Quarter Sessions—August 1816)

James Seeley	Acquitted	Jonas Taylor	12 months
James Burroughs	,,	William Seeley	,, ,,
James Howard	,,	Jeremiah Osborn	,, ,,

TABLE 6

Labourers charged with causing a riot at Ratlesden (Bury Quarter Sessions—August 1816)

Name	Sentence	Name	Sentence
Robert Leader	2 years	John Folkerd	Bound over
Hy. Poole	1 year	Benjamin Buxton	,,
Robt. Durham	,,	John Chinery	,,
John Smith	,,	Robt. Osborn	,,
John Abbott	,,	Martin Moore (or Mono)	,,
William Howe	,,	Jno. Bird	,,
William Hall		Geo. King (or Hong)	,,
William Richer (or Richor)	Discharged in own recognizance	Thos. Mattock (or Mattocks)	,,
Robt. Gladwell	,,	John Steggles	,,
Robt. Folkerd (or Folkard)	,,	Robt. Cobble (or Cobbold)	,,
R. (or William) Nunn	,,	Charles Cobble (or Cobbold)	,,
John Ward		Robt. Baxter	,,
John Golding	not guilty	Jas. Button (or Burton)	,,
William Underwood	,, ,,	Thos. Durham	,,
Ezekiel Buxton	bound over	Benj. Steggles	,,
Mesach Moore	,, ,,	James Clover	,,
James Southgate	,, ,,		

TABLE 7

Names of prisoners involved at Brandon—16/17th May 1816. (*Those tried at the Summer Assizes, Bury, July 1817)

Name	Occupation	Name	Occupation
William Arnold*	Shoemaker	Mingay Rampling*	Labourer
Henry Spendlove*	Labourer	Ann Folkes*	Labouring Woman
Helen Dyer*	Married Woman	John Crane	Labourer
Robert Field	Labourer	William Peverett*	Labourer
Porter Talbot*	Labourer	William Clark	Labourer
James Wiggar*	Labourer		

TABLE 8

Names of Labourers charged with rioting at Swaffham Bulbeck
(Cambridge Quarter Sessions)

William Ullyar	6 months	Joseph Flack	3 months
James Thompson	,, ,,	John Fordham	,, ,,
John Stickwood	,, ,,	William Clements	,, ,,

TABLE 9

Names of Labourers charged with Riot and misdemeanour at Hitcham (late 1816)
(Bury Quarter Sessions—January 1817)

Jos. Grimwood	3 months	Francis Wright	Bound over
Thos. Preston	,, ,,	William Banks	,, ,,
Rich. Daking	Bound over	Jno. Downing	,, ,,
Jos. Haste	,, ,,		

TABLE 10

Names of Labourers charged with destroying a threshing machine belonging to William Burlingham at Hockham—19th May 1816
(Norfolk Quarter Sessions—July 1816)

John Abery (or Abry)	12 months	Peter Palmer jun. (24)	3 months
Peter Palmer sen. (63)	3 months	James Bailey	12 months

TABLE 11

Names of Labourers charged with breaking a threshing machine belonging to William Sach at Layer Bretton

Thos. Gooday	12 months	Thos. Wade	6 months
Jas. Gooday	6 months	Robt. Beercroft (or Beechcroft)	,, ,,
William Row	12 months	Jas. Howard	,, ,,

TABLE 12

Labourers charged at the Ipswich Quarter Sessions, Summer 1815, with rioting and smashing machinery, the property of John Roper at Holbrook, 2nd August 1816

Daniel Grimwood	Robert Page
Thomas Seager	— Sells
Joseph Cook	John Driver
Martin Gosling	Jerry Lucas
Robert Payne	— Bayley
Samuel Page	S. Turner

TABLE 13

Labourers charged (Woodbridge Quarter Sessions, January 1816) with riot and machine smashing in Kenton and Mon-Soham

Edmund Prime	12 months	William Barker	12 months
William Garnham	,, ,,	Thomas Stevens	,, ,,
William Bannister	,, ,,	John Brunwin	6 months
John Abbott	,, ,,		

INDEX

INDEX